Homecoming

Homecoming

A guided journal to lead
you back to nature

MELISSA HARRISON

WEIDENFELD & NICOLSON

First published in Great Britain in 2024 by Weidenfeld & Nicolson,
an imprint of The Orion Publishing Group Ltd
Carmelite House, 50 Victoria Embankment
London EC4Y 0DZ

An Hachette UK Company

1 3 5 7 9 10 8 6 4 2

ISBN (Hardback) 978 1 3996 1877 9

Colour origination by f1 Colour, London
Printed in China by C&C Offset Printing Co. Ltd

www.weidenfeldandnicolson.co.uk
www.orionbooks.co.uk

CONTENTS

INTRODUCTION

Hi, how are you doing? I'm so glad you're here. Welcome to your own, personal nature journal, and to a new – yet age-old – way of being in the world. It can be hard to know what to prioritise, what with so many things fighting for our attention, so many supposed routes to wellness or fulfilment, happiness or wealth. People find something that works for them, be it exercise, meditation, CBD or crypto, and then sell it to others as the be-all and end-all.

Is connection to nature any different? Isn't it just another niche life hack? You could say I'm biased, because it's become so central to me, but it's a more effective and well-proven intervention than almost any other route to a better life. Humans didn't evolve indoors with air con, disinfectant, electric light and heating. We evolved in natural environments, so every aspect of our functioning has been fine-tuned for millennia by the life forms and natural processes around us. Far from being some kind of fad, reconnecting to nature returns us to a more normal, balanced and elementary state.

Studies have shown that hospital patients healed faster from surgery and needed less pain relief if they had a view through a window of a natural scene, rather than a brick wall; and that a friendly bacteria found in soil triggers the release of serotonin, affecting the brain in a similar way to antidepressants. Touching a piece of wood, as opposed to metal, calms the prefrontal cortex and results in greater parasympathetic nervous activity, markers for physiological relaxation; smelling petrichor, the fragrance released by rain on dry earth, has a similarly mood-boosting effect. Spending time in natural environments improves working memory, cognitive flexibility and attentional control, while walking in a wood improves cardiovascular and metabolic health, as well as improving immune function – the list goes on and on.[1] And it shouldn't really come as a surprise.

Like every other living thing, human bodies and minds have been refined for millennia by contact with myriad aspects of the natural world, yet in the last couple of centuries – the blink of an eye in evolutionary terms – we've made it possible to live a life that's disconnected from our environment, and we are now discovering that this disconnection seems to cause us a range of physical and psychological harms. The effects can be powerful over time, yet they're subtle: they can creep up on us slowly, so that we often don't know what it is that we lack.

That's what happened to me in my twenties, when I was living in central London – and for the most part, if I'm honest, I didn't consciously miss nature at all. I was too busy working, going out, building a life and having fun, and I let the rich, thriving world that I'd felt so attached to in childhood slip away, unremarked. Even the seasons faded into near-insignificance: for years, I thought of them mostly in terms of what to wear and whether to take an umbrella to work. But a hunger was growing inside me, a feeling of loss

....

1   If you'd like to learn more about the science of nature connectedness, I can thoroughly recommend *Losing Eden: Why Our Minds Need the Wild* by Lucy Jones and *Reconnection: Fixing Our Broken Relationship with Nature* by Miles Richardson. You'll find more reading recommendations in the Resources section at the back of this book.

and disconnection, and eventually I realised that what I needed was green and growing things.

The process of reconnecting was slow and instinctive, rather than deliberate. I moved to a rented flat in Streatham with a scrappy back garden and began to note down when the plants in it flowered, so I could add things I bought in trays from the supermarket and always have something nice to look at. While looking for garden ideas, I began to notice the seasonal timings of natural phenomena in the streets around me, like magnolia trees in spring and honesty seed pods in autumn, and when my husband and I adopted a rescue dog I found out where all the local parks were, and began to visit them daily, getting to know them in all weathers and times of the year. I also bought an entry-level 'proper' camera at around this time and began to learn how to use it. I can see now that, led by some obscure instinct for wholeness, I was relearning how to look, and in doing so, reminding myself of something really crucial: that nature operates on a repeating cycle. Each month brings new things to look out for, many of which can be experienced only briefly – but which return again the following year, to be enjoyed once more.

I *knew* this, of course – just as you do – but somehow I'd forgotten. The natural world had become a sort of backdrop: rarely in focus long enough for me to really engage with it. I'd lost sight of how rich it is – yes, even in cities! – and how fleeting its events are. The absolute joy, the preciousness of it, comes from the realisation that there might only be a few days in which – as one example out of thousands – the cherry blossom is at its most ludicrously pink and frilly: a day of heavy rain and it's on the pavement, gone again for another year. The goal is to enjoy each phenomenon in the moment, as it unfolds – and on *its* terms, not mine or yours: a form of mindfulness, of course, though I hadn't heard the word then. Weirdly, I began to find it relieving not to have everything I wanted, when I wanted it – and nowadays I *love* the fact that I'm not in charge. The natural world doesn't operate on demand, and that simple fact alone does us good.

Tuning back into nature and the rhythm of the seasons was deeply enriching as well as life-altering on what I'd go so far as to call an existential level, and I tried to write about it in my first novel, *Clay*. The wise and indomitable Sophia tells her granddaughter, Daisy: 'the things you really bother with in life loom large, you see, so you do well to choose them wisely… some things help you grow, and some are just empty, like too many sweets.' Just as who you choose to follow on social media determines the character of your timeline, what you choose to notice and care about determines how nourishing your daily reality is.

I found that instead of time being a linear plod to an invisible horizon, it became a series of cycles, always with something to look forward to or to enjoy again. Now I feel anchored by time and within the seasons in a way that feels utterly transformative. Add to that the sheer difference in my day-to-day reality now that it's populated, in the foreground, by living things I notice and care about – and which I can help – and I've come to understand experientially what the science shows: that this kind of natural, temporal awareness is a crucial part of living well.

But if a voice in your head (or in your family!) tells you the natural world is dirty, practise gently challenging it. Only around one in a billion microbes are harmful to humans, and more kinds of pathogens live inside your home than outdoors. And the most important thing to remember is this: instead of harming you, regular contact with the natural world *actively boosts your immune system*, making you healthier and more able to fight off disease.

One more thing – perhaps the most important of all. Reconnecting to nature isn't about fleeting, one-off acts designed to give you a 'dose' while leaving the rest of your life unchanged; it's about building a lifelong, meaningful relationship. And that relationship shouldn't be extractive: after all, treating the natural world as something that exists purely for our benefit is what's led to many of the problems we face today.

So, for everything good you experience in the course of the coming year, I hope that you'll discover a deep desire to offer protection and custodianship to the world around you in return. If I'm honest, that's the main reason I wrote this book: because, as Sir David Attenborough has said, 'No one will protect what they don't care about, and no one will care about what they have never experienced.' I look at climate change, which is happening now, as a kind of bottleneck: not all of the creatures we share our world with will make it through. To maximise the number of species that survive what's to come we *all* need to be on board, using whatever tools we each have – and with love and wonder as our driving force.

I believe that an imaginative and emotional connection to nature produces two sets of benefits: to us, and to the natural world itself.

HOW TO USE THIS BOOK

This journal is designed to be a year-long course in noticing, one that will plug you back into the rhythm of the seasons across the British Isles in a way that you can carry forward into the rest of your life. Each month, I'll tell you some of the stories, small and large, unfolding all around you – whether you live in the heart of a city or deepest countryside.

But this isn't just a reading book, it's a *doing* book – and that's really important. After all, the thing that has the power to change your life isn't within these pages, it's out there: in your garden, on your street, in your local park, through your car window and on your weekend walks. So, to help you bring it into your everyday life, I invite you to write down in this journal the very best thing you experience in nature each day, whether it's a bird, a cloud formation, an unusual-looking paw print or a fragrance that stops you in your tracks. You can start in any month, in any year, and continue on round to where you began.

If you find yourself thinking, *But writing in books is wrong! I don't think I'm going to do it,* please imagine me furrowing my brow at you sternly. I really, *really* want you to write in this book in order for you to get the full benefit of our year-long journey. Research by Miles Richardson, who is an actual Professor of Human Factors and Nature Connectedness (!) at the University of Derby and the author of *Reconnection: Fixing Our Broken Relationship with Nature*, has shown that powerful and long-lasting increases in nature connectedness come from the act of reflective writing – even if it's only a few words. So please, as well as reading this book, I beg of you: write in it! That's what it's been designed for.

For each month, I've chosen some key things to look out for and enjoy. For the most part, I've concentrated on what's common and close at hand so that you can follow along, wherever you live, but there are a few ideas for things you can look for if you're willing to travel. However, not everything can be found in every location: there are no snakes or moles in Ireland; you'll find stag beetles in the Southeast but are very unlikely to see one in Wales, and you're more likely to hear a cuckoo in Scotland than Surrey. So, don't be limited by my suggestions: your goal is to discover and connect with the nearby nature you have, whatever it might be.

Each month there'll also be a 'bird by ear': an opportunity to learn to detect the presence of a bird by its song, call or other sound, if you'd like to (and it's completely OK if you don't). I'd recommend reading my description while playing the song, call or other sound on a reputable site such as www.xeno-canto.org or via the brilliant Merlin app (see Resources), then going out with your ears primed to hear it. When you do, try to get 'eyes on' to the bird in question, as that, I find, helps the sound and ID to marry up properly and stick in your head.

In writing this book, I haven't tried to be comprehensive; I've focused on the plants and creatures I love and want to tell you about, and which I hope will be relatively easy for you to find. But there's so much more going on around you than there is space for in this book, so please, don't confine yourself to my checklists and suggestions: get curious about everything you notice. What is it? What's it up to? Why is it *here* and not *there*? How can you give it a helping hand?

This book doesn't prioritise rarities, native species or even, in the strict sense, *wild*life: I've included some garden plants like wisteria, that you might see on neighbours' house fronts, activities and processes to look out for on the farmland many of us have become so disconnected from, and some introduced species, like the parakeets that have made London their home and are fast fanning their viridian wings across the rest of the UK. That said, here and there I've also made mention of some uncommon creatures, like nightingales, that can only be found in particular places, or whose numbers have fallen to levels that mean many of us today will find them hard to see or hear. Despite that, they form part of the shared cultural heritage of everyone who lives on these islands, appearing in stories, songs and folklore, and you'll see them crop up on TV and perhaps on your socials, too. You deserve to know what we're losing, so you can go and find it, should you want to – and while there's still a chance to turn things around.

But as you establish this new habit, please don't be hard on yourself. At first you might not be able to identify the things you see and hear easily – but that's because you're learning, not because you're no good at it. See p. 13 for some helpful pointers on using identification apps, websites, social media and books, but mostly, just give yourself a break: it takes time to build the brain architecture to tell a robin's song from a blackbird's, but it does happen once you set aside enough synapses for it and build a habit of noticing. You'd be amazed how many friends of mine began this journey unable to tell cow parsley from hogweed, or a swift in flight from a swallow, and who now tell me it seems so obvious that they can't remember a time when they didn't know. It'll happen to you, too – but until then just enjoy the noticing, because the other stuff will come.

And remember, when you go for a walk, stopping and waiting and looking and listening are all part of reconnecting to nature – even if you don't manage to see the mystery creature or identify the bird this time. Allow yourself to be comfortable with uncertainty, doubt and occasional frustration: all key aspects of relating to the unpredictable, enriching, non-human world.

Finally, you might miss a day of this journal, or a few days, or even a few weeks – and that's all right: life happens, and nature will always welcome you back home whenever you're ready. There really is no failing at this, because the journey is the goal.

OBLIGATORY DISCLAIMER

The timings of seasonal events differ across the British Isles, often by as much as a month; what's more, the dates on which things occur can change from one year to the next as a result of weather conditions. Added to that, cities produce microclimates in which plants may flower earlier or for longer than in open countryside, or which allow migratory birds to spend the winter instead of leaving for warmer climes; plus, some formerly reliable occurrences are shifting, prompted by our warming climate. All of this means that I can't tell you *exactly* when you'll see your first orange-tip butterfly of the year or hear your last swift. The prompts in this book are there as a guide, but what's really important is for you to determine your own local timings, so you can find your feet and begin to compare one year to the next.

In each month there are key things for you to look and listen out for, and tick off; but if you experience one of those things in a different month, just tick it off there (and if you don't see it this year at all, you'll have another chance next year).

You'll see that one or two things to look out for include a space in which you can write the date. These are particularly key moments in the year, the timings of which can be usefully compared from one year to the next. You'll probably see people getting excited about those things on social media: a welcoming, rewarding and refreshingly wholesome form of online chatter that I invite you now to join in with, or simply eavesdrop on, if you prefer. In the Resources section at the back of the book you'll find some suggestions for people to follow online who will truly rewild your timeline, along with books, websites and apps that'll help you tune in to everything from the aurora borealis to common fungi, from dead animals to the moon.

CAN I SEE SOME ID?

The first thing to say about identification is that you don't
have to bother with it if you don't want to: it's perfectly
OK simply to appreciate the beauty of wildflowers or enjoy
listening to birdsong without working out the correct names
for everything. For some people, in fact, it can produce
anxiety, or act as a barrier to pleasure, and if that's you, listen
to that instinct: it's *far* more important that you connect
imaginatively and emotionally with nature than that you learn
the genus or species of something.

Me, I like to know the names: it feels like being
introduced. I'm not someone who keeps a 'Life List' of the
species I've recorded, though I know that brings others a
great deal of satisfaction, but if I have a name for something,
I can look it up to find out more about it: what it needs,
how it behaves, whether it's doing well or is in trouble, and
perhaps how I can help. It lends richness to the world when
I can differentiate the things living in it; when, instead of
there being *some* birds in my garden, I can tell you
that there are, say, eight kinds I see regularly, and
a couple more who pop in from time to time;
when I can recognise most of the plants
growing in my tiny strip of verge and know
that more kinds grow here than when I
moved in; when I can find out why I see
different insect species down by the river
than live in the churchyard. The richer

 the natural world gets in my mind, due to telling one thing from another, the more gloriously its details pop and the greater the joy I get from it all.

On a scale of 0 to 10, where 0 is a nature newbie and 10 is a proper expert, I'm probably about a 6, hoping to make 7 (I would have marked myself higher once, because I didn't realise how far beyond me the scale went). I've amassed a good library of identification books and do a lot of looking things up, and I learn as much as I can from generous experts willing to share their knowledge, but I've no formal training in this field. What I am, though, is an excellent noticer, and I'm curious, and although I forget some of the things I learn, some of it sticks. With each year that passes I add a little more knowledge to my store – and that's how I know that you can, too.

At first, you'll find it hard to see the difference between things, just as I did – even when it's pointed out. It takes time for your brain to get granular enough to tell apart the similarly sized and coloured buttercup from cinquefoil, or hear the difference between the two-note songs of a great tit and a chiffchaff. And this lack of granularity at the start is worth bearing in mind for two reasons: firstly, because it'll change, so don't be discouraged; and secondly, as a guard against premature certainty. When I first started learning about nature, I confidently misidentified almost everything left, right and centre, simply because I *didn't know how much I didn't know*. And because certainty kills off curiosity, that held me back from discovering more. When I spot something unfamiliar now, I try to hold my guesses lightly, and then I check it as thoroughly as I can in my reference books at home.

Trusted sources

I've mentioned books because, even in the digital era – perhaps *especially* in the digital era – they are important. The information in a reputable botany or ornithology ID book, or in one of the Field Studies Council's excellent fold-out guides, will have been produced and rigorously checked by experts, and can be relied on; similarly, the information on websites such as that of Butterfly Conservation, or the RSPB. However, the terminology around species identification can seem opaque at first and you might need to put some time in to work out how to use the charts and keys; I'm very aware that this can be a barrier to the kind of instant answers we all crave and which you'll probably seek out.

But the fact is, some of the newer digital sources just aren't reliable. I've found that species are routinely misidentified online on everything from social media and image sharing sites to reputable picture libraries. Identifications are made online without key information such as where something was seen or at which time of year, and errors go uncorrected. These are often then multiplied unchecked from one source across several sites – and thus, the ID apps that scrape the internet for training data.

Even when asking real humans for help online, a complicating factor is people's general helpfulness: everyone wants to suggest a good answer when someone asks what something is, but as I've already mentioned, many of us aren't aware of how much we don't know – for example, how many close mimics a flying insect has, or that a family of plants is 'taxonomically intractable' (i.e. a hot mess, even for botanists). Although I love chatting to other nature lovers online about what something might be, I've learnt to take strangers' well-meant 'reckons' with a large pinch of salt, unless I can be sure they really are an expert in the relevant field.

ID apps

All that being said, the digital realm is – let's be honest – where most of us are going to go to get answers, not least because it lives in our phones. And one of the ways in which we're increasingly accessing information is via those identification apps I mentioned, or Google Lens, or the reverse image search function that now comes built in to some mobile operating systems. Smart ID functionality offers identification suggestions based on photos or sounds, and while some are absolutely brilliant – the free Merlin Bird ID app, for example – others, such as Visual Look Up on iOS, trained on Siri Knowledge and 'similar pictures found online' – leave a *lot* to be desired. My worry is we don't always know enough to know when we're being told the wrong thing, and that hinders our own learning processes as well as building in errors that then get baked into the system as we add more incorrect info to the pool of it circulating online.

The answer? Look at the training data. The reason Merlin is so good at recognising birdsong is that it was built by a reputable educational organisation (the Cornell Lab of Ornithology) and its training data comes from expert birders: people using the eBird network around the world. The free German app Flora Incognita is also impressively reliable when it comes to recognising wildflowers; again, it's a scientific research project with training data provided and continually updated by botanists, citizen scientists and researchers. Importantly, both apps take into account your location and the time of year in generating a result. In contrast to these complex scientific projects, there are commercial ID apps popping up daily, trained purely on web 'reckons' and with no greater goal than extracting a couple of quid from users whose knowledge they will thoroughly set back.

So, when you're choosing a 'smart' identification app, read up about it on its website rather than just choosing the first one that pops up on your app store or whichever one bombards you with ads on Instagram. Go for one that's built on a database of expert, frequently updated training data (Merlin comes with large data packs tailored for each region) and which uses your location to tailor its suggestions – I can't tell you how many times Visual Look Up on my iPhone has confidently identified North American species when shown quite common UK plants.

Most importantly, treat the answers it gives you as suggestions: even the mighty Merlin has blind spots (or deaf ears), confusing, for instance, the '*hweet*' call of a chaffinch (extremely common) and a common redstart (less so); I try always to get 'eyes on' before believing in a bird call it has identified, and never add a species to a conservation or citizen science database without being 100 per cent sure. Your job, when you ask an app and it gives you an answer, is to investigate further – perhaps via a trusted website such as the British Trust for Ornithology (www.bto.org), Butterfly Conservation (www.butterfly-conservation.org) or a book. Does the plant or creature even occur in the place in which you saw it? Are you likely to see or hear it at this time of year, or is it absent/in hibernation? How common is it, really? (Although we all want to see something unusual, the truth is that rarities are just that: rare).

A case in point: walking on Whitehawk Hill in Brighton, I found a bright pink flowering plant that looked like a gladiolus. Had I believed Visual Look Up on my phone I would have put it down as *Gladiolus illyricus*, the UK's only native gladiolus, but this, as I discovered from the Botanical Society of Britain and Ireland's online Plant Atlas, (www.plantatlas2020.org) is vanishingly rare and confined to the New Forest. Meanwhile, my Flora Incognita app had it as *Gladiolus communis*, a Mediterranean introduction that sometimes naturalises on waste ground, and this seemed both less exciting but more likely. That evening I appealed for help on social media and was sent an article by Anthony Hamilton, formerly Senior Lecturer in Plant Sciences at the University of East London and a renowned *Gladiolus* expert, and this confirmed it as *Gladiolus communis* subsp. *byzantinus*, not native but the subject of much interest and study. Incidents like these are a reminder of how much I still don't know, and that helps me not to jump to too-easy conclusions, especially when aided by AI.

I write all this knowing that the technological landscape is changing so fast that by the time you read this it might be irrelevant. That's where books and scholarly publications have the edge, either by themselves or as the second stage after using a reputable app, and if you discover that you do enjoy identifying things, you'll find some reliable guides in the Resources section at the back of this book. Many can be bought second-hand for not much at all, especially as most of us don't need to have the very latest edition – my much-used copy of *The Wild Flower Key* by Francis Rose was last revised in 2006. While things like distribution and population size may change over time, and some areas, like gull identification, have been transformed by advances in science, in most cases the basic facts about what something looks and sounds like will still be correct whether the book you're looking it up in is from three or thirty years ago.

KIT

What do you need to connect to nature? Absolutely nothing. Look out of the window and enjoy what you see; watch it change from one season to the next, and try to work out what lives there, and what it's up to. Look up at the trees as you pass underneath them, or peer into other people's front gardens; take a route through a park when you can, and pay close, kind attention to how the things you experience make you feel. Use your imagination, your heart and all your senses; get into the habit of noticing, and at the end of each day, write down in this journal the thing you most enjoyed. That's pretty much it.

There are some add-ons you might enjoy using as you tune yourself back in to nature, but they're by no means necessary. Jammed into my pockets or somewhere about my person are usually a **dog poo bag,**[2] a **small ruler** and a **mini multitool**, all of which can be useful when it comes to bringing things home for investigation or taking a photo for later ID; I've got friends who are into insects who carry a small **pocket magnifier**, too. I pop my ruler (it's from the Filofax I had when I was seventeen) into any photos of poo, eggs or prints, for scale; if I don't have it, I include

2 Or a sandwich bag. Also useful for taking other people's litter home. My rule is that you're not allowed to moan about it if you're going to walk past it – one reason I pick rubbish up on most walks. Don't fall into the trap of thinking there's so much that you might as well not bother: every Fruit Shoot bottle, cellophane fag packet sleeve and Monster Energy can counts.

my own hand, foot or finger, laid flat on the ground at the same distance from the lens as the mystery object. I promise, the first thing any expert will ask you, on being shown your blurry images, is how big it was – and you need to be able to tell them. And if you're sharing photos online and asking for help, make sure to say where the photo was taken and at what time of year.

If you're thinking of exploring nature in new or unfamiliar places, I can thoroughly recommend the **Ordnance Survey (OS) app**. You can subscribe for a whole year or just buy access for a month, or if you buy one of their paper maps you get a code which gives you access to the digital version. There are three excellent things about the OS app: firstly, it uses GPS to locate you on a detailed map which, when you zoom in, shows you all the rights of way in green – these are paths that anyone is allowed to walk on, so you know you're not trespassing. Secondly, when I say 'detailed' I mean *really* detailed. As opposed to other UK maps, 'Premium Topo' OS maps show woods, ponds, interesting ruins, earthworks, standing stones, old tracks and more: as you walk you can consult it to work out what's around you, making the world approximately 300 per cent more interesting – which, frankly, is brilliant. And thirdly, you can find walks in it that other people have done, showing the length, the average time it'll take and the elevation (how uphill and downhill it'll be). Do be sensible, though: using a navigation app for short walks in ordinary places is fine – just make sure you have a backup battery for your phone, as GPS can be power-hungry – but if you're going anywhere really challenging you *must* learn how to use a paper map and compass first.

You may also wish to try the free **Encounter app** I'm in the process of making. It's a nature journal that lives on your phone: you can make notes on it, take photos of the things you see, create audio recordings and receive reminders

and prompts from me that will alert
you to things you can look out for, all
year round.

Magic bins talk

Once, on quite a tired day, I couldn't think of the word
for binoculars and came up with 'far-lookers', and that's what
they are to me now. I *love* my far-lookers and sling them
around my neck nearly every time I leave the house, just in
case. I'll never forget the time I saw a small, squat silhouette
sitting on an overhead cable which, through my trusty bins,
turned out not to be a starling but a furious-looking little owl
staring back at me. However, you certainly don't *need* a pair
to enjoy the natural world.

   If you do choose to borrow or buy some binoculars, the
best advice I can give you is to go smaller rather than bigger,
and buy second-hand. Not only is it more sustainable, and
cheaper, it's just not necessary to have brand-new bins in
the way it might be with, say, a laptop, which needs to keep
up with constant updates. Then, think about how you'll use
them: are you really going to go out regularly in poor light
conditions? If not, you don't need huge lenses that can gather
all the available light, and this will save you weight (and cost).
Honestly, the number of friends I have who like Big Bins
(and cannot lie) but never use them because they're unwieldy
and uncomfortable to carry. It's such a waste.

   My Nikon Monarch 7 8x30s are compact and light; I
replaced the uncomfy strap with a cheap neoprene one from
eBay and I wear them slung cross-body, which can be more
comfortable for women than having them banging about on
your chest as you walk. I bought them over the phone, as
reconditioned, from a specialist camera and binocular retailer

who I trusted to describe their condition accurately, and when I scratched a lens I sent them to Nikon for repair. The rubber casing is a bit battered-looking, but I paid about half of what they would have cost new, and because of that saving I was able to get a better, lighter pair than I otherwise would have been able to afford.

Just a note, though: people don't realise that using binoculars takes practice. At first, you'll find it hard to get the object you want in view and focus quickly, and that'll feel frustrating, but with the right pair and a little determination, you'll find it becomes second nature pretty fast.

KIT CHECKLIST

☐ Dog poo bag or sandwich bag

☐ Small ruler or something for scale

☐ Mini multitool

☐ Pocket magnifier

☐ Navigation app

☐ BONUS ITEM: Binoculars

January

*Once upon a time it was
January, and nothing
had yet unfolded, and
everything that would
happen was yet to come*

I'd like to tell you a story. It's an old one – perhaps the oldest there is – and it's one you probably know already, though if you're like me, at some point you'll have lost sight of its once-familiar shape. Now, in the cold, still point that is January, it's time to orient ourselves to it again.

You may know this tale in two ways: from half-remembered homework, barely thought of since school days; and deep in every synapse, in the very marrow of your bones. Both ways are liable to getting a little hazy, given everything. But once we've followed nature through the course of a year and tuned back into its ancient rhythm, it will anchor you again to the living world of which you are a part. You'll never find yourself adrift from it again.

On these isles, it's dark when your alarm goes off in January, dark when you finish work for the day: only a third of each 24-hour cycle is spent in daylight, give or take.[1] Even when the sun is up it stays low in the sky, never reaching the 60 per cent elevation it does in midsummer, and this means it generates less heat. The earth under your feet has been cooling down since last summer, and at this point in the year it's cold: no longer radiating warmth to boost the atmospheric temperatures. No wonder it can freeze overnight in January. Without residual warmth in the soil and only a weak, low, short-lived winter sun, there's little to keep us warm.

Plants draw energy from the sun, so in January, at our latitude, there's not much growing – a good thing, given that ground frost can fatally damage tender, unprotected plant tissue. Species that have been on these

---

1   Roughly speaking, a January day in London at the start of the month equates to 7 hours 55 minutes of light and just over 9 hours by the month's end; Scotland and northern England, being further from the equator, have shorter days than the south in winter, but longer in summer.

isles for millennia have had to find ways to deal with winter: jettisoning leaves and foliage, retreating underground until the following year or dying off altogether, having reproduced and left their seeds to start anew in spring. Meanwhile, evergreens have evolved tough, frost-proof foliage, while winter specialists like snowdrops (more on those in a moment) draw on energy stored in their bulbs from the previous year.

Most insects eat plants, whether that's nectar and pollen, leaves or sap. At this time of year, the dramatic lack of plant growth means there's hardly any food for them – added to which are the dangers to their small, cold-blooded bodies of a hard frost or snow. So they've had to evolve ways to survive winter, too: you'll doubtless have noticed how few there are around compared with June, say, or July. Many, like grasshoppers, will live out their life cycle in the warmer months and then die off in autumn, leaving eggs or larvae behind them that will overwinter and become adults the following year; some, like ladybirds, will find a sheltered spot and become dormant for the winter; others, like honeybees, store up food which they can live on when there's nothing around to eat. A few, like the **red admiral butterfly**, migrate, though climate change is helping them to overwinter here now in increasing numbers, which led in part to a 400 per cent boom in population in the summer of 2023. On a sunny January day you might see a red admiral butterfly on the wing, tempted out from a shed or outbuilding.

What is the knock-on effect of hardly any insects out flying or foraging? There are hardly any of the creatures that rely on them for food. Bats and hedgehogs disappear to hibernate; insect-eating birds like swifts, swallows and flycatchers have migrated south to warmer and more insect-friendly climes and won't return until April or May; others, like blackbirds, skylarks and dunnocks, change their diet, switching from invertebrates to weed seeds and berries, and this is why it's so crucial to let weeds grow and then leave them over winter, and to allow berry-bearing hedges and trees to set fruit.

But the cycle of plant growth is dictated not only by soil temperature but by day length, and increasing periods of light in January – whatever the weather – is something we can rely on. As the month progresses, the days slowly get longer: at first by just over a minute per 24-hour cycle, but by the end of January the sun's putting in an extra 3 minutes 16 seconds of work a day. That's more and more energy that can be converted to plant growth, and while most – apart from some bulbs, unfurling in the darkness – won't do much yet in case of sudden frosts, they have an internal biological clock, just like we do, that knows what's coming. Preparations for growth are being made.

The days will continue to lengthen right up until Midsummer's Day, which falls in the second half of June when we get nearly 17 hours of sunlight per 24 hours from the sun around 60 degrees overhead, making the rays more concentrated and powerful: a double whammy of stronger sunlight for longer each day. By that point, plants will be taking advantage of all that energy by going absolutely bonkers in a mad rush to claim space and reproduce. After midsummer, as the days slowly shorten and they complete their reproductive cycle, they'll slow down again; some, like annuals and second-season biennials, will completely die away; others, for instance the bulbous plants and perennials, will lay down energy in their root systems and then let their top growth desiccate; some, like cereal crops and fruit trees, will put their energies into producing fruits and seeds. Insects, likewise, will slowly decline and many adults will be killed off at last by the first frost of winter. I sometimes think of the year's natural activity as a series of bell curves, with light levels preceding plant growth, plants preceding insect activity, insects preceding birds and average temperatures peaking after light levels have started to decline, with everything falling away again slowly to the near-flatline of December and January.

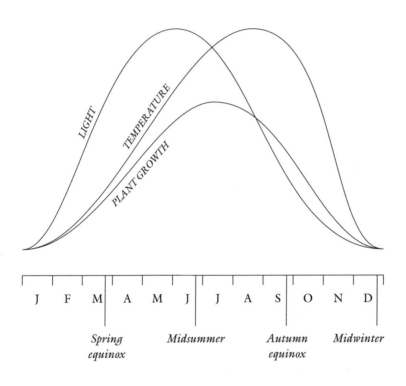

But what makes each season different from the previous year's is the way weather conditions modify the daylight. When it's cloudy, less of the sun's light gets through to help plants grow, so a sunny spring means more leafy growth, sooner, and thus more insects out earlier – including more caterpillars, which act as moist baby food for many birds. A dry spell means flowering plants will produce less nectar, and that will affect the insects that rely on them for energy, and in turn, the creatures that prey on them. Drought can also limit plant growth, as does persistently low soil temperatures, while changeable conditions can be lethal: a warm spell can lure plants out of dormancy and into growth, only for a sudden cold snap to kill that new growth off; if this happens to, say, the blossom buds on fruit trees it can mean they're not able to flower and later set fruit, and there'll be fewer food sources for thrushes and blackbirds the following winter. Meanwhile, a winter without a proper freeze can mean that pathogens that usually die off in cold weather are free to multiply, leading to more pests and diseases the following spring.

As you can see, each year unfolds at its own unique pace and pattern, often (but not always) differently in different parts of the UK – and each season tells a story that can knock on to affect the years to come. But behind the normal seasonal variation, climate breakdown is altering the likelihood of certain weather patterns, and consequently, the life cycles of everything from bee-eaters to bees. The long-standing correlation between fresh new plant growth, the caterpillar explosion and birds' breeding season is one of the key mechanisms underpinning the natural cycle of the year, so the fact that spring is arriving earlier is a huge concern. Some birds seem to be breeding earlier, so they can continue to take advantage of the caterpillars; others, like the fast-declining cuckoo, aren't able to shift the timing of their migration to this country. Satellite tracking data has shown that they need to fuel up before their arduous journey, which means waiting for an insect explosion at their wintering grounds, triggered by the spring rains. What's more, many bees are now waking from hibernation too early, when little is in flower and there isn't enough nectar or pollen for them to eat.

Right now, though, it's the bleak midwinter and we have no idea what sort of spring it's going to be. In January we watch, and wait, and read the signs, hoping that spring, when it comes, will bring kind weather – including enough (but not too much) rain.

In recent years a new ritual has come to mark the start of the year. The **New Year Plant Hunt** began in 2012 and is now firmly established in the UK's thriving citizen science calendar. Citizen science projects offer meaningful and satisfying ways to get outside and start your journey of noticing; it's usually easy to take part and I'll be including several on our journey through the year. For this one, participants spend three hours on any day between New Year's Eve and January 1st recording any wild or naturalised plants (i.e. growing in the wild, rather than in gardens) that are in bloom in their local area, then send their findings to the Botanical Society of Britain and Ireland. Once the results are in, they're shown on an interactive map and used by scientists to track the effects of climate change and weather fluctuations on the natural world. Sign up at www.bsbi.org/new-year-plant-hunt or follow along online using the hashtag #newyearplanthunt.

While most flowers in the New Year Plant Hunt will be outliers, somehow blooming, against the odds, at the wrong time of year, the **snowdrop** is the classic flower of January, perfectly adapted to midwinter conditions. Given there's little sun, they use energy stored in their bulbs to get going, and while their nodding white bells may look delicate, their tough shoots are specially adapted to push up through frozen soil. Cleverly, snowdrops also contain their own antifreeze: a hard frost will make them droop temporarily, but unlike tender species their cell walls aren't damaged by the ice crystals and they soon spring up again. Because they bloom when there aren't many invertebrates around, they don't need to be pollinated to reproduce; instead, the bulbs multiply underground. However, if it's mild and a bee happens to emerge early, they will visit snowdrops in search of food; then, if it *is* pollinated, the plant will produce a seed with a fatty coating that's irresistible to ants. They'll take it away to their burrow, thus planting it and establishing an entirely new bulb.

The three other plants I regularly see in bloom in January are all yellow. Spiny, prickly **gorse**, which likes sandy heaths, uplands and coastal areas, is known for putting out its coconut-scented flowers in any and every month, hence the slightly bawdy old saying, 'When gorse is out of bloom, kissing is out of season'. **Winter aconites** are another January bloomer: low-growing gold buttons also known as 'choirboys' for the green ruff around their necks. Finally, pretty, pale yellow **primroses** are really a flower of February and March, but I have seen them out in January, particularly in warm, sheltered spots. They really do feel like a promise of spring.

Truly resplendent in January, though, are the mosses: without roots that penetrate the soil, they need damp conditions to stay alive, so are at their best in the wet winter months – you'll barely notice them in summer, so the time to enjoy them is now. We have over a thousand species of moss in this country; learning to recognise them all would be a life's work, but not knowing what they are doesn't make them any less lovely to look at. Woodlands in January are often shag-carpeted in species of feather-moss, or clothed with the tiny emerald stars of bank haircap, the trunks of trees grey-green, too, with algae, particularly on the shady side. But the moss I love the most is the humble **wall screw moss**: neat green pincushions that often appear on walls, roof tiles and gravestones, and which feel familiar to me from childhood, each one a tiny islet emerging from a stony sea. To reproduce, it sends up amber-coloured capsules of spores held on fine threads, like a little grove of trees on a grassy mound.

Generally speaking, this month there are only a few birds you're likely to hear singing properly (as opposed to the general tweeting birds produce as alarm calls or to keep in contact with one another). Unlike most birds, robins and **wrens** sing all year round, while – if you're especially fortunate – you might hear the gorgeous, repeated phrases of a **song thrush**, which sound to me like someone calling a register, repeating each name a few times and then moving on to the next: '*Timothy, Timothy, Timothy, Timothy. Liv, Liv, Liv. Archie, Archie, Archie, Archie, Archie…*' and so on. These blackbird-sized birds with spotty chests are known for occasionally singing extremely loudly in the depths of winter, often because they've found a good tree or bush with tasty berries on it and they're declaring that it's theirs and can't be stolen by other thrushes, blackbirds or our winter visitors from further north, like redwings, fieldfares and waxwings.

Unless it's a particularly warm, sunny January, birds are likely to be in survival mode, rather than breeding, and many will spend the short daylight hours in loose, mixed-species flocks while they try to forage enough food to get them through each long, cold night. But one species in particular can often be seen looking for nest sites this month: the **ring-necked parakeet**.[2] Thought to have bred from escaped pets, these loud, adaptable, confident green parrots are recent additions to our breeding birds, and because they evolved somewhere with a different climate pattern (Pakistan and northern India) their instinct to breed kicks in at a slightly different time than that of our native birds. First making their home in London and then spreading into the Southeast, they can now be found in most counties – particularly in cities and suburban areas. Research is ongoing into whether they might outcompete birds like nuthatches and great spotted woodpeckers for cavities in trees to nest in; if you have them near you, look out for them investigating potential dwelling places this month, and sometimes quarrelling with grey squirrels for the best nesting holes.

In some cultures, the first full moon of the year is called the **Wolf Moon**, and I'd recommend you make a note to see it (in fact, while you're at it, look up all the year's full moons and note them in this journal so you can plan some night walks, or add them into your calendar app). In winter, the moon rises very high in the sky, which means we view it through less of our atmosphere, so it appears whiter, its light colder than at other times of the year. I love to walk at night and plan my walks around full moons so I don't need to use a torch, which reduces night vision and scares all the wildlife away.

Finally, if you're out after dark this month, keep an eye (and an ear) out for **foxes**: January is breeding season. You might hear the unearthly screams a vixen makes to attract male foxes, or even see

---

2 Also known as the rose-ringed parakeet.

a gathering of males around a female, ready to fight for the right to mate.

Now you're ready to start making your own nature notes: remember, try to write down the best thing you experience in the natural world every day, but don't worry if you miss a day, or a week, or longer. Just come back to this journal when you can.

Each day, note down the very best thing you experienced in the natural world.

Date

Date

Date

Date

Date

Date

Red admiral on the wing Date: _____

BIRD BY EAR

Wrens produce 10dB of sound from a 10g body, far more per gram than most other, bigger birds, and that alone helps us to distinguish their loud song. Each burst – already very fast at 36 notes per second – includes a manic trill that sounds like someone operating a tiny machine gun just inches from your ear. Looking like walnut-sized teapots, wrens are shy and hard to see, but once you tune in to their song, you'll realise they're everywhere: in fact, they're our most numerous wild species. Listen to their song on an app (such as the Merlin app listed in the Resources section) or online, and then head out for a walk. January is a good time to hear them; as the year progresses, more and more species will start singing, and they'll be harder to pick out.

☐ *Primrose in bloom* Date: _____

When taking a photo of an object to identify later, always include something for scale – ideally a ruler, but a finger or pen will do. Place it at the same distance from the lens as your mystery item.

Wall screw moss

  ☐ *A carpet of snowdrops* ☐ *Winter aconites*

Date

Date

Date

Date

Date

Date

☐ *Coconut-smelling gorse*

Date

Date

Date

Date

Date

Date

🔍 ☐ *Wall screw moss*   ☐ *A vixen screaming*

Foxes breed in January, in city and in countryside

Each day, note down the very best thing you saw in nature. Research shows that nature connectedness is boosted by building a habit of reflective writing, even if it's only a few words.

☐ *A wren singing*

For such a small bird, wrens have a big voice!

Make a note of the dates of the full moons for the next twelve months: if the skies are clear, those nights, and the three or so either side, will be good for walking. Note the dates of the Geminids and Perseids meteor showers, too.

Parakeets investigating nest holes

Date

Date

Date

Date

Date

Date

☐ *Wolf Moon*

Date

Date

Date

Snowdrops: demure yet tough

🔍 *BONUS* ☐ *Took part in BSBI's New Year Plant Hunt*

Date

Date

Date

Date

If you have a favourite tree, start giving it a surreptitious (or not so surreptitious) #patoflove when you pass. This hashtag was started by The Tree Council a few years ago (@TiCLme), and the science backs it up: touching timber is relaxing. It might also feel encouraging for the tree!

☐ *Song thrush singing*

February

As the short days inevitably lengthen, the living world uses each day's extra light to quietly, tentatively get into gear

If January was a bare and darkened stage, in February the first, promising stirrings can be detected in the wings. Make no mistake: it's still firmly winter, and in some years February can feel even colder, darker, wetter or snowier than the first weeks of the year; as someone whose birthday falls in this month, I am very familiar with how dim and sometimes endless it can feel. However, it is an undeniable fact that it is usually in February that Things Start Happening, and the more familiar you get with the grand, unfolding pageant of the year, the more you'll learn to feel and see winter loosening its hold – even if the temperature remains low.

In some years – depending on weather conditions and food availability – the birds that have spent the winter with us, such as redwings, fieldfares and punky, Mohican-headed waxwings (if we've had a 'waxwing winter', see p. 222) begin to depart in February, usually slipping away at night. They'll be heading back to their breeding territories of Finland, Sweden, Norway and Iceland, ready to find a mate, and by the end of April they'll probably all be gone. If you've got any near you – gorging on the berries on supermarket car park cotoneasters, perhaps, or feeding on open fields – make sure to enjoy them while you can.

As for our resident birds, it's sometimes said that they pair up for the coming year on Valentine's Day. It's a nice thought, and while it's obviously not something to be taken entirely seriously, it's certainly true that February can bring an increase in **courtship behaviour** in many of our most familiar birds, behaviour that can be better seen for the fact that there is so little foliage for them to hide behind. Whenever you see your local robins, sparrows and blackbirds, stop for a moment and try to get a look at what they're doing: you might see females begging for food by crouching and shivering their wings, or the males bringing them tasty titbits; males might shadow females, keeping them constantly in sight; or you might see birds preening one another as a form of pair bonding.

Spring is the season for birdsong. It's easy to forget this, but by high summer, when the breeding season ends, most birds will have stopped singing again, and you'll miss them. So keep your ears peeled when you're in the garden or local park: song (rather than contact or alarm calls) begins to increase this month as male birds begin to feel the urge to establish a territory and attract a mate. By the time May comes, birdsong will be at its peak.

It's usually about now, on a cold, sunny day, that I'll hear **drumming** from areas of deciduous woodland. The sound has become one of my most satisfying 'firsts' of the year. Great spotted woodpeckers choose hollow, dead or rotten wood for its greater resonance, hammering on it with their beaks to claim a territory and communicate with one another. They nest in holes in trees, including in some city parks, and often reuse existing cavities; however, if they do excavate a new hole, the sound is a much slower tapping than the staccato vibration of the territorial drum. Numbers of this smart black, white and red bird have been on the rise for a while now, and they've also expanded their range north and west, hopping across to Ireland in 2006 and then breeding successfully both north and south of the border. It's cheering to see (and hear!) them doing so well.

Towards the end of this month you might see a **male greenfinch** performing a display flight: a roughly sparrow-sized bird, green up close, circling with slow wingbeats at about house-roof level and singing as it flies. However, numbers of this lovely little finch have been decimated in recent years by a nasty disease that emerged in 2005. Though there are no records of it affecting humans, trichomonosis is now known to be badly affecting other garden birds too, including chaffinches, goldfinches and great tits. Its spread is being assisted by bird feeders and bird baths, so if you have either, remember to clean them regularly with extremely diluted bleach.

In February you might even see **birds with bits of nesting material in their beaks**, which means that now is the time to put up a **nest box**, if you'd like to, or clean out any existing ones ready for them to be used again. Birds' nests are protected by law: they mustn't be disturbed, moved or destroyed while they're being built or in use, so from now until around the end of August you must be really careful about cutting hedges, felling trees or doing any building work where birds nest, or you may face prosecution.

If you live in or near the countryside, or visit there this month, you might see rooks returning to their communal **rookeries**, usually in clumps of tall trees, and rebuilding old nests. Some rookeries are known to be well over a century old, and at one time it was thought that they conferred a desirable air of tradition and antiquity to one's country pile: the nouveau riche were known to try and move nests to trees close to their new-build mansions in the hopes of establishing a new site, and some people still believe that if rooks abandon a rookery, disaster will follow. Obviously, interfering with nests is a terrible idea, but I strongly approve of people being proud of their local wildlife instead of seeing everything non-human as an inconvenience.

Rooks look (and sound) a lot like crows but they live in large, loose groups, and if you see them up close their beaks are pale grey, rather than black. Garrulous and highly intelligent, they are very messy nesters and can be highly competitive over who gets the best twigs, so if you hear a commotion above you and see twigs and bird poo all over the ground, look up. If the rooks are building, spring isn't too far away.

Rooks aren't the only reason to look up this month. It might seem as though winter is the worst time of year to be noticing trees, what with them largely being bare, but before they come into leaf we get a window to look at the form their branches take, and this can be a really good way to identify them. For instance: ash trees have a habit of sending the ends of their branches down and then up again, like beckoning fingers, giving the whole tree a different shape to, say, an oak. And in February you'll start to see **pointed black buds on the end of ash twigs**, looking at first like little black hooves on the grey leg of a deer, then swelling to become fat and sticky and bursting open in a few weeks' time into small, green and burgundy, gill-like flowers, which will be followed by the leaves.

It's important to enjoy our tall, stately ash trees while we can, as a new tree disease called chalara, or ash dieback, may soon mean the loss of this common and familiar species from our parks, gardens and countryside. We lost all our elms a generation ago, and many of us (including me) know their shape now only from old landscape paintings and the few that survive around Brighton. There's lots of research being done into whether some strains of ash may prove to be disease-resistant – unlike the elm, it's a very genetically diverse tree, being able to cross-pollinate, self-pollinate and even change sex – but the picture at the moment is bleak. Ash trees have been here for such a long time that they've developed relationships with hundreds of other species – almost as many as the oak has – so their loss will have a terrible knock-on effect on our biodiversity. We'll also lose the shifting, dappled shade their pinnate leaves create in summer, the rattling sound of their dry bunches of seeds ('ash keys') and the source of the phrase 'ash blonde', which relates to the pale colour of their wood. Trees are deeply rooted in human culture, as well as in our landscapes. Of course, they also do crucial work in terms of our climate, but it's important not to see them – or anything in nature – simply as machines for our use.

Also widespread, but thankfully not threatened, hazels are a short, shrubby tree with almost round leaves, when they come. Before the leaves, hazels put out long, dangly **catkins** on bare twigs, and they are a classic sign of spring. Also known as 'lambs' tails', they're long, greeny-gold and often appear in bunches; at first, they look smooth and grey, but on a warm February day the scales will open and show the yellow pollen inside. If you spot a hazel, make a note of where you found it: if you go back in autumn you can snack on the brown, ripe hazelnuts. However, take note: if the catkin tree you're looking at also has what look like tiny brown pine cones on it, it's not a hazel but an alder, a damp-loving, short-lived pioneer species which tends to hold its branches out horizontally, and whose wood turns bright red when cut and exposed to air. No nuts in autumn, either.

In February I like to peer into other people's front gardens for witch hazels (no relation to the hazel) and **Japanese quinces**, both of which flower around now. Japanese quinces – also known as *Chaenomeles* – come in various shades of pink and pinky-red, are often used in hedges, and can be breathtaking: the small, waxy flowers appear on bare, dark branches and look like a Japanese woodcut. **Witch hazel flowers** are equally eye-catching: weird little twizzles on a slim, bare tree, like pinky-orange fireworks or bright pencil sharpenings, and with the most extraordinary perfume.

Neither are native,[1] as is often (but not always) the case with plants that flower earlier, or later, than the rest.

In cultivated places like parks, gardens and, often, graveyards, **crocuses** start blooming now in shades of lilac, purple and yellow, and always remind me of clutches of baby birds opening their beaks to the sky. They originate in the Mediterranean, North Africa and parts of Asia, and are a great source of nectar and pollen for **buff-tailed bumblebee queens**, emerging from the disused mouse or vole burrows in which they've spent the winter, as well as any early honeybees. Honeybees can be tempted out by a sunny morning but will need to fuel up quickly because a dip in temperature in the afternoon can prove fatal – so if you can, planting a few sources of early nectar will really help. Crocuses open in sunlight and close in shade, so if you buy a few bulbs (available cheaply from garden centres and supermarkets in autumn), plant them where they'll get direct sun in the daytime in February, or pollinators might struggle to get to the nectar.

This month the snowdrops in gardens, parks and wild woodlands are joined by **lesser celandines**, a pretty, native wildflower that looks a bit like a buttercup, only with pointed petals instead of rounded. It particularly likes damp spots and will continue to bloom into April. Here and there in shady

---

1 'Native' is a slightly woolly term. It can mean those species which called these islands home while they were still attached to the European mainland, or which arrived here a little later but under their own steam; it's also widely used to mean those species which were not introduced by humans. In ecological terms, the value of native species is not intrinsic, it is simply due to the fact that extended amounts of time spent in a particular environment allow species to coevolve, form relationships and become useful to one another. Some new arrivals, whether from other countries or from the UK to elsewhere, cause problems as they lack sufficient controls in their host country (i.e. other organisms that eat them). However, other introduced species can find perfect ecological niches or quickly prove valuable.

places the green, rolled **spears of cuckoo pint**[2] or **lords-and-ladies**, will poke up through the cold soil, ready to unfurl, followed by a white, lily-like flower in April and May, and then a spike of bright orange berries in autumn.

Lambing time, for most sheep farmers, begins around now. They will have put the rams in with the ewes back in autumn, often staggering the process so all the lambs aren't born at once, as it's hard, stressful work for farmers; the lambs will be sold on in five to eight months' time, depending on how big they've grown. Look out for them in the countryside, wobbly-legged and curious, headbutting their patient mothers for milk. And yes, **spring lambs** really do gambol, chasing one another and bouncing around as if they're on springs.

While you're out staring at fields, look for **molehills**, too – unless you're in Ireland, that is, which has no moles, weasels or – famously – snakes. Moles are active all year round, but in dry weather the worms and invertebrates they eat tend to go deeper into the ground, and the moles follow suit. In winter and spring, when the ground is wet, they often hunt nearer the surface, kicking up the soil they excavate to make molehills. I've seen moles above ground a few times, and it always make me smile: they're like dark grey, velvety sausages with feet. Their front paws are pink spades, their eyes can barely be seen and their soft fur has no 'nap', by which I mean it doesn't grow in any particular direction – something that makes it easier for them to trundle backwards in tunnels. How brilliant is that?

....

2   Several plants and even insects are named after cuckoos, which arrive here in spring – when *arum maculatum* flowers. As for 'pint', it's from an old-fashioned word, 'pintle', which meant 'penis': inside the white sheath (called a 'spathe') of the flower is a phallic-shaped 'spadix'. *Arum maculatum*'s other names include priest's pintle, the willy lily, soldiers' diddies and finally – and I apologise in advance – dog's cock.

Last month we enjoyed the first full moon of the year, the high, white Wolf Moon. Now it's the time for the **Campaign to Protect Rural England's (CPRE's) annual Star Count**, usually held in February. This project aims to track and measure light pollution, known to be one of the leading drivers of insect decline as well as having negative impacts on a vast range of other organisms. Don't worry, you don't have to count all the stars in the sky: merely those in the constellation of Orion, the hunter with his belt and sword, which is super-easy to find (see p. 244).

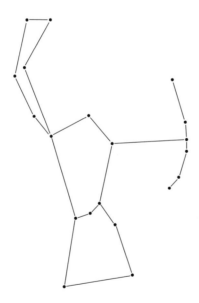

Each day, note down the very best thing you experienced in the natural world.

Date

Date

Date

Date

Date

Date

🔍 ☐ *Great spotted woodpecker drumming* Date: _____

BIRD BY EAR

The great spotted woodpecker uses its beak to produce a sharp, short '*drrrrrrr*' lasting up to a second with a strong reverb on it, usually repeated at intervals. Both sexes drum to announce and defend territory, their beaks striking wood (or anything resonant – they've been known to drum on metal poles!) at up to forty beats per second. We have three woodpeckers in the UK, but it'll be the great spotted woodpecker you hear; the lesser spotted has been lost from most of the country, and the green woodpecker barely ever drums, communicating largely via a loud, laughing call (the green woodpecker used to be called a 'Yaffle' based on this very sound).

☐ *Hazel catkins releasing pollen* Date: _____

When looking things up, always be sure to use your location and the date to check whether the species in question is likely to exist when and where you are.

Hazel catkins

 ☐ *Pair bonding/courtship behaviour in birds*   ☐ *Birds preparing to nest*

Date

Date

Date

Date

Date

Date

☐ *Greenfinch display flight*   ☐ *Rookery reoccupied*

Date

Date

Date

Date

Date

Date

🔍 ☐ *Ash twigs with sticky black buds* ☐ *Japanese quince in bloom*

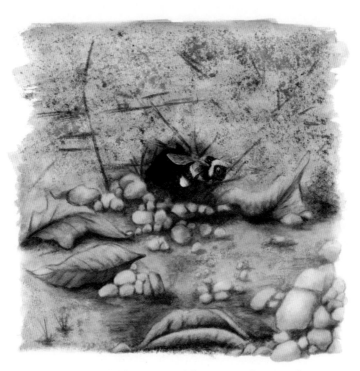

Buff-tailed bumblebee queens hibernate underground

Keep your ears peeled! On a walk in
Cumbria I heard a faint sound behind me:
a red squirrel was running along the top of the
drystone wall I'd just climbed over. If I'd had my
earbuds in I'd have had no idea it was there.

☐ *Witch hazel's fragrant, fizzy flowers*   ☐ *Arum's rolled spears*

Gifts of food can help couples bond

Rewild your timeline: follow some friendly and interesting nature people and fill your feed with seasonal pics and info. You'll find a list of suggestions on p. 287.

Crocuses – any colour ☐ Lesser celandines ☐

Date

Date

Date

Date

Date

Date

☐ *Fresh molehills*

Date

Date

Arum's rolled leaves break ground, spearing up between celandines

BONUS ☐ Lambs ☐ Buff-tailed bumblebee queen

Date

Date

Date

*Consider joining your local Wildlife Trust,
particularly if you have kids. They have lots of
outdoor activities to get involved with, but are also
a great source of news about your nearby nature.*

☐ *Took part in CPRE's Star Count*   ☐ *Put up a nest box*

March

This month brings the vernal equinox, one of the year's four turning points. Insects begin to be seen again in greater numbers and plants put on growth

OK, now we're getting somewhere. It's March, and at last – *at last!* – spring is really starting to happen. Sure, some years this month can still be really cold, not to mention windy, wet and miserable. But around the 21st comes the equinox, when day and night are of equal length: from that day on, light overtakes darkness in each 24-hour cycle.

Plants respond to the increasing day length by putting on growth, a response called photoperiodism. As they grow, and, hopefully, the temperature begins to rise from its midwinter depths, insects begin to be seen again, for example, the four species of butterfly which pass the winter as hibernating adults: the sulphur-yellow **brimstone**, ragged-winged **comma**, pretty **small tortoiseshell** and impressively-eyed **peacock**. The red admiral butterfly can be seen too – large numbers often arrive from North Africa and the Med in spring. The females then lay eggs here, leading to a second generation in summer which, having bred and laid eggs, would historically die off when temperatures fell; however, this species is benefitting from a warming climate and more and more are managing to overwinter here.

As insect numbers swell, providing extra food sources for birds, birds breed and more arrive here from foreign shores, staying with us until the weather cools, plants stop growing and insect numbers fall again. This yearly pulse, this ancient natural rhythm, is the vital heartbeat that underpins so many of our seasonal processes. I find it deeply grounding and enriching to see and feel it happen each year. Observing this natural rhythm helps me to tell apart simple yearly variations from signs of disruption through climate change.

There are two main waves of avian migration that dramatically change the make up of the UK's birdlife: one in spring, starting this month, and another in autumn. From now until May, dozens of species will appear, from little willow warblers, dragonfly-hunting hobbies and chirruping, fork-tailed swallows, to huge, fish-eating ospreys. Others will leave: redwings, fieldfares and waxwings come here each autumn to escape colder, harsher winters further north, and leave again in spring. Several species of geese, too, depart around this time, and you might spot them flying overhead in long, straggling lines or Vs, known as **'skeins'**.

But there's one incoming migrant I get very excited about this month, despite it being extremely common, not much to look at and the owner of perhaps the most thoroughly boring song of any of our birds. I'd like to introduce you to the chiffchaff.

Now, the chiffchaff is, in birding terminology, a classic 'LBJ' or 'little brown job' – though to be more accurate, it's robin-sized and olive green, with a paler chest and tummy, and it has the narrow beak characteristic of insect-eaters. Why do I get excited about something so nondescript? And why do so many other people cheerlead for it every March? Because it's the first of the common summer migrants to arrive back on our shores, usually aided by a southerly wind (so keep an eye on the weather forecast) – and whether or not it's beaten some years by a wheatear or sand martin doesn't actually matter because it's so widespread and so vocal that it's the summer visitor most of us will notice first, right across the UK. The **first song of the chiffchaff** means that spring is firmly here and summer's just around the corner: I've been stopped on the street by people pointing out one singing, and given the news by my postie along with my junk mail and bills. So, towards the end of the month start listening out for a persistent, rhythmical '*dink – dink – dink*' like a bored toddler with a one-note xylophone – a sound that will continue all spring and summer, only stopping in September when most of them make off for warmer climes again.

Chiffchaffs will be our 'bird by ear' for April, by which time they should have arrived across the country and be singing strongly everywhere.

But a much more beautiful and complex song – in fact, my favourite song of all the UK's birds – is that of the good old blackbird. This is a species that stays with us year-round, but the males only sing during their breeding season, usually – though this can vary a little from year to year and place to place – from March to around the end of July, depending on the weather and where you live. For the rest of the year you'll mostly only hear their alarm calls, let out when strictly necessary – including the explosive series of clucks and shrieks they fire off if you startle them, and as they fly away.

I've sometimes heard my **first blackbird song of the year** in February, but most often it's in early March. Once they're in full song they have a lovely habit of singing in the late afternoon, moving between tall perches around their territory, such as a chimney, an overhead cable, an aerial or a tree – and this, rather usefully, makes it easy to spot them, as I find that seeing a bird actually singing is by far the best way to commit the sound to memory. Try to get your ear in this month, and then make a note to enjoy each and every performance. The song may not be as extraordinary as a nightingale's, but everyone can hear one, and if I could only listen to one bird for the rest of my life, this would be it.

It can be possible to tell one blackbird's song from another's: as they get older they'll often incorporate interesting sounds they've heard into their repertoires to show how experienced and thus, what a good survivor they are. Most years, if I really make the effort to listen and notice, I can tell 'my' garden blackbird from his nearest rival. As I write this, I'm listening to one singing from the gable end of next door's roof. He has a sort of crazy, bubbling flourish he adds to the end of every few phrases, quite unlike any other male blackbirds nearby.

The scruffy feral pigeons found in towns can breed year-round, but there's a clear uptick in **pigeon courtship behaviour** around now. The males puff themselves up and follow the females around, ducking and bowing. You might even see them mate. These are highly intelligent and resourceful birds, not to mention amazing long-distance navigators and acrobatic fliers, and I have no time for those who call them 'flying rats', or worse. I find it interesting that the types of creatures we express the most hatred for – like rats, cockroaches, feral pigeons and grey squirrels – are the most like humans: numerous, clever, adaptable generalists who somehow manage to thrive in urban environments, and who have learnt to get by on what we throw away. It seems to me that what we are really feeling about them is projected disgust: difficult feelings about ourselves that we direct elsewhere as a way of dealing with the discomfort.

March is a good time to start keeping an eye out for the uprush of vegetation which will soon start to gather pace. Find a sunny, neglected bit of verge, the edge of a park or some weedy waste ground near you – a place you pass often, rather than somewhere you'll have to make a special trip to see – and make a note of how tall the greenery is: we'll have another look in May.

As we discovered in January, if you look really hard you can usually find something managing to flower, even in the depths of winter and even if there's nothing around to pollinate it. But March is when wildflowers reliably start to bloom, cheering up parks, pavements and verges, and bringing a bit of colour back to the world. Look out for pale yellow **primroses**, while humble **daisies** and **dandelions** usually get going, especially in warm, sunny weather; I really love **red dead-nettle**, too, which can be spectacular on areas of waste ground. Like its bigger cousin, white dead-nettle, the leaves of this lovely little wildflower look like nettles but don't sting. It's brilliant for bees, especially the early-awakening, long-tongued species that can reach inside its purple flowers.

But March is truly the month of the **daffodil**, and you'll see them absolutely all over the place. Some people are a bit sniffy about them, particularly the very bright yellow kind, preferring the paler varieties or their close cousins, the paper-white narcissus. It's true that the plant they originated from, the wild daffodil – which can still be found in some parts of the countryside – is prettier and more delicate. But honestly? By the end of winter, I'm ready for a bit of brashness and a good cheering up. Plus, chilly bees often warm themselves up in the shelter of their trumpets, which in sunshine can be several degrees warmer than the surrounding air.

The *Prunus* tree species now begin to edge quietly into bloom, their timing a little later the further north you are – as is the case with many spring phenomena. Well before the frilly pink blossoms of the Japanese ornamental cherries comes the humble cherry plum with its simple white flowers which appear before the leaves. Next – sometimes as early as February – comes the closely related blackthorn, often seen as a hedging plant: it's well described for its long, hard, incredibly sharp spines, the scourge of country dwellers' car tyres. Later in the year its blossoms will become dark blue sloes, unbelievably sour to taste but excellent for making sloe gin – so if you find a blackthorn this month, make a note to return. Wild cherry joins the party last, usually in April; its flowers are held in small clusters, but otherwise these **three**

Prunus **species** can be tricky to tell apart. However, they're all equally uplifting: whichever one you spot in flower, it's a sign that the sap is rising and spring is under way.

When I was a kid, March meant you'd regularly start seeing (and hearing!) **hedgehogs** out and about after dark, following their winter hibernation, but their numbers have fallen to such a degree that many people will spend their whole lives without seeing one in the wild, unless it happens to be dead on a road. Mind you, those that are left can be hard to see, being nocturnal, which is where a wildlife camera can come in very handy; there's an excellent website included in the Resources section at the back of the book if you'd like to get one. But another good way of finding out if hogs are about is by keeping your eyes peeled for their poos. Imagine if you squeezed out about 2–5cm of toothpaste, but it was black, firm and slightly glittery: that's a **hedgehog poo**. The glitter effect comes from the munched-up exoskeletons of all the beetles and other invertebrates they eat.

We know that they're eaten by badgers, but the two have coexisted for millennia without hedgehogs becoming extinct, so badger numbers aren't the whole picture when it comes to hedgehog decline. The widespread use of slug pellets has had an impact, as has the increasing numbers (and speed) of cars on the road, but perhaps most catastrophic has been the loss of tangly, untidy, insect-rich habitat for them to live in. We've tidied and divided everything up so much that it's hard for a creature like a hedgehog, which needs lots of habitat to hunt for food in (even more now that there are fewer insects about) to establish good enough numbers to cope with the other pressures on it, which is entirely on us, and something we need to change. Having said all that, they are still around – albeit in dramatically reduced numbers – and we should enjoy them while we can. If you think they're visiting your garden you could set up a trailcam to find out; alternatively, look online to see if there's a local hedgehog group you can join. Lots of neighbourhoods have plans in place to try and protect them, including helping to make sure people's gardens are welcoming places for them by creating safe spots for hibernation or making holes in the bottoms of fences so they can move around.

Hedgehogs hibernate over winter and wake around now in order to keep in step with the fall and rise in invertebrate numbers caused by annual temperature changes. **Bats** are exactly the same: they hibernate in winter when there's little or nothing for them to eat, and emerge when the world warms a little and insects are back on the wing. I usually see my first bat of the year this month; when I was younger I might have heard its ultrasonic squeaks before I saw it, but like most people over about twenty, I've lost that register now. Look out for them at dusk, flickering silently overhead, and if you can, put up a bat box: going by the droppings on the windowsill beneath it, mine was occupied the first winter I put it up. The other good thing you can do is reduce the number of outdoor lights as much as possible. Light pollution disrupts invertebrates' life cycles in multiple ways – as well as those of birds, bats and many other species – and is a key driver of the crash in insect numbers.

It's hard to tell which type of bat you've encountered without a specialist detector: these convert their clicks and squeaks to audible range and analyse the pitch. You can try one out by booking on to a walk organised by your local Wildlife Trust. In the 1990s it was found that the bat we'd previously just called the pipistrelle was in fact two species, now called the common and soprano pipistrelle. This discovery was first made due to the fact that they had different frequency echolocation calls, and it was then found that the two did not interbreed. In evolutionary terms, they are in the process of diverging.

In the arable farmland around where I live, in Suffolk, I sometimes see **hares chasing and boxing** in pairs and groups as early as March; this courtship behaviour continues through spring, but as grass and cereal crops grow taller, the hares (much bigger than rabbits, with black-tipped ears) are harder to spot. What I see far less of around here than I'd like to, though, is **spawn**, whether belonging to frogs (laid in a big, blobby mass), toad (laid in long strings) or newt (eggs laid individually). Knowing what I'm like, my neighbours will often tell me when they first see some in their garden ponds, but I rarely now find it in 'wild' bodies of water; however, the fact that there's usually frogspawn in the Barbican Wildlife Garden, right in the heart of London's Square Mile, makes me enormously happy. Few things feel more spring-like than spawn, with its promise of transformation. It's no surprise that children, who are also in the process of changing from one state to another, find it so endlessly fascinating.

Each day, note down the very best thing you experienced in the natural world.

Date

Date

Date

Date

Date

Date

🔍 ☐ *Newly arrived chiffchaff singing* Date: _____

BIRD BY EAR

The song of the blackbird is a rounded, fluty warble with plenty of melodic variation, slow enough for each note to be heard and copied, if you wished. He incorporates long, thoughtful-seeming pauses between phrases during which he listens out for any rivals; you might hear another singing distantly in these pauses and realise you're witnessing a sing-off. Compare the song of a blackbird to that of a robin by going online or using an ID app (see Resources). The blackbird's song is a rich and cheerful tenor, as opposed to the robin's reedier, higher, somewhat wistful soprano that often ends on a wavering, uncertain note.

☐ *First blackbird's song* Date: _____   ☐ *Bat on the wing* Date: _____

From March to July, keep dogs on leads on beaches, farmland and uplands. Even if they're not interested in birds, they will disturb ground-nesters like skylarks and lapwings, and could be the factor that causes a nest to be abandoned. Some nature reserves may not allow dogs, for this reason.

Red dead-nettle

 ☐ *Spawn* Date: _____   ☐ *First brimstone butterfly* Date: _____

Date

Date

Date

Date

Date

Date

☐ *Skein of geese*　　☐ *Feral pigeons' courtship displays*　　☐ *Red dead-nettle*

Date

Date

Date

Date

Date

Date

🔍 ☐ Prunus *blossom (wild cherry, blackthorn or cherry plum)*

Blackbirds sing in spring and early summer

Worried about where you can walk? On Ordnance Survey maps (paper, online or on the OS app) rights of way are marked in green, so you always know you're not trespassing.

Butterflies: ☐ *Small tortoiseshell* ☐ *Comma* ☐ *Peacock*

Male frogs are generally smaller than females.
Their spawn is laid in large clumps.

*The more good experiences you have while enjoying
the natural world the stronger the positive association
you'll build. Before long, just stepping out of
your front door will give you a feeling of joy.*

 ☐ *Daisies* ☐ *Dandelions*

Date

Date

Date

Date

Date

Date

☐ *Primroses* ☐ *Daffodils*

Date

Date

Date

The sulphur-yellow brimstone butterfly

BONUS ☐ *Hedgehog out and about*   ☐ *Hedgehog poo*

Date

Date

Date

Date

People can be super-helpful online – even when they don't know much more than you do. When it comes to identification, check if someone really is an expert before taking their word for it.

☐ *Hares chasing and boxing*

April

The month of buds and
blossom, when the grass greens
to growth, wildflowers bloom
and spring gets its legs under
it and starts surging forth

Wherever you are in April, whether town or countryside, look up and out: one by one you'll see the bigger trees edging into leaf, 'like something almost being said', as the poet Philip Larkin wrote. Meanwhile, on roadside verges, spring wildflowers like **speedwell**, **herb robert** (which smells of mice) and **garlic mustard**, aka jack-by-the-hedge (which smells of garlic), are popping up all over the place, while in woods, ditches and along the margins of farmland fields, primroses are giving way to their cousins, the tall-stemmed **cowslips**. The **first dandelion clocks** appear, and in a warm, sunny April you might even see your first ox-eye daisy of the year (aka dog daisies or marguerites: imagine an ordinary daisy but on steroids) – although for me that usually happens in May.

Stinging nettles – a really important plant for butterflies, moths and ladybirds, as well as for birds, which eat its seeds later in the year – really starts to put on growth in April, as does **goosegrass**, also known as 'cleavers' and, regrettably, 'sticky willy', a fast-growing, scrambling, sticky weed with tiny hooks on both surfaces of its leaves that help it ratchet up and over other plants, and round burrs that catch on animals' fur (and human clothes) in order to spread its seed around. It has a habit of forming tall, dense thickets which then die back in late summer to leave a crumbly, ghostly tracery, like something from Miss Havisham's abode.

Grass, too, turns lush and green about now, and in parts of the country where there's dairy farming you'll see **cows reappearing in the fields** after a winter spent under cover eating dried and fermented forage harvested last year. Rabbits begin breeding as soon as there's enough new grass for weaned **baby bunnies** to eat, and from gardens everywhere, April often brings the first sound of **mowers** and strimmers. However, there's a growing understanding that wilder lawns really benefit wildlife, and lots of gardeners now are delaying their first cut and signing up instead to 'No Mow May'.

I don't have a lawn, only a scrap of verge about 4m long and 40cm wide. I let it grow tall and tangly, and over the last few years more and more species have moved in: ribwort plantain, red dead-nettle, a single common daisy, common mouse-ear chickweed, hedgerow cranesbill, false oat-grass, ox-eye daisies. Studies show that greater plant diversity boosts both invertebrate diversity and invertebrate numbers, and as we've learnt, more insects mean more of everything else – and when I part the stems I see spiders, froghoppers, grasshopper nymphs, craneflies, aphids, ants and other little critters I can't name. That all adds up to more life that my tiny, richly fruitful verge is contributing to the local ecosystem. I would rather have that any day of the week than a closely shorn strip.

One of the most unmissable spectacles of the month is that of English **bluebells**. Around half the world's population of this gorgeous wildflower can be found in the UK, and they were thought to arrive just after the last Ice Age. While the odd one sometimes flowers in March, late April into early May is when woods the length and breadth of Britain become carpeted in the most incredible shade of ultraviolet, a colour that photographs never quite seem to capture – just as they cannot capture the intoxicating smell. It doesn't stop anyone (including me) from trying, though, and the internet is flooded with bluebell images every April, something of which I'm pretty sure I'll never tire.

We think of English bluebells as growing in woods, but that's not always the case and there are several upland areas, such as on Dartmoor, where sheets of them can be seen. It's not the shade they need so much as soil that doesn't dry out in summer, a task that can be performed by plants like bracken and heather. They also need the ground they live in to be left undisturbed.

In urban areas it's common to see Spanish bluebells in parks and gardens, as well as hybrids between the Spanish and English species. Spanish bluebells are bigger and meatier, with wider leaves; they're also scentless, and instead of the little florets hanging to the same side of a drooping stem like a shepherd's crook, they appear all the way around an upright, central stalk like a candelabra. They're still pretty to look at, but if you ask me they're not a patch on the wild thing, and they can be thugs in gardens. Wild bluebells, however, are protected by law, so make sure not to pick them or dig them up; happily, the bulbs aren't too expensive and can be ordered online if you'd like to have some in your garden. Like snowdrops, they're best planted 'in the green' (i.e. with foliage attached) after flowering in spring – but if you're itching to grow something now and you have room for a large pot or grow bag, tomato seedlings are easily and cheaply picked up from supermarkets and garden centres. I do a couple of the cherry types each year. This is also the month to buy **sweet pea seedlings**, a tray of which can be picked up for a couple of quid. Pop them in the ground somewhere sunny where they'll have something they can twine their fine tendrils around to climb up, like a wire mesh fence or a cane wigwam, and keep them *very* well-watered (by which I mean, every couple of days). You'll thank me come July, I promise.

In town gardens, **magnolia trees** can be spectacular in April. These non-native trees have silvery bark and put out huge, waxy, white or pink and white flowers well before their leaves open. Magnolias are an incredibly ancient species, so old that they evolved before bees even existed. Their flowers are pollinated by beetles instead.

You'll also see a lot of brightly coloured tulips in flower this month and next. These have been carefully bred to come into bloom at different points in spring, so they're not something I use to track the year's progress – I just really enjoy seeing them. The time to plant tulip bulbs, if you'd like to, is in autumn, so I'll remind you about it then. Ten or twelve in a pot protected from squirrels will provide a lovely pop of colour by your front door next spring.

As we learnt in the previous chapter, our native wild cherry, or 'gean', puts out its simple white flowers around now; its nectar and, later, its fruits are important for wildlife. But it's the fluffy pink or white, many-petalled kind of cherry you'll see much more of in towns and cities as they make a well-behaved street tree: one that looks pretty, won't grow too big, won't drop slippery fruit on the pavement (sadly, most **ornamental cherries** are sterile) or need regular pruning; and it's these which hit peak frothiness this month. In Japan, *hanami,* or cherry blossom viewing, is an important spring rite, and it goes without saying that photos of cherry trees in flower against blue April skies are a staple of springtime social media feeds.

At this time of year, as their food sources increase, more and more insects are either waking from hibernation, emerging from cocoons as new adults, or hatching out from eggs. I start looking out for **seven-spot ladybirds** around now – by which I mean active ones moving around on vegetation, rather than tucked away in a corner of my window or dormant in my shed. It's important to count the spots on ladybirds in order to know which type you're looking at; in 2004 a new kind, called a harlequin, became established in England and is now spreading further, and research is ongoing to work out whether it's likely to cause problems. Even if it doesn't, it's the native kind we're interested in as a way to mark the seasons: creatures that have lived in the same spot for a long time tend to have closely adapted their life cycles to local weather and seasonal patterns, and so are a more reliable indicator of any change.

It's a good time of year to spot newly emerged **red mason bees**: a small, gingery, solitary pollinator that makes its nest in holes in sunny brickwork or in the hollow stems of plants. This kind of bee is a vital pollinator and will readily move into a bee hotel, either home-made or shop-bought. I have a bee nesting box on the back wall of my house which can be opened up and reassembled: later in the year I'll carefully remove the tiny cocoons using a dry paintbrush and store them in a small carton in my shed until they're ready to hatch the following spring, when I'll bring the carton out and prop the lid open slightly so they can fly off. Meanwhile, I clean out the nesting box, let it dry and put it back together again, ready for a new set of guests. Doing this keeps the baby bees safe from parasites.

It's still early in the year for most butterflies with the exception of those we met last month, who passed the winter as adults. But there are a couple that buck the trend. The **holly blue**, which is most numerous in the south of England, has two generations per year, and the spring cohort start to be seen on the wing around now. Bear in mind that the UK has several blue butterflies (there's also the common blue, which is the most widespread, the small blue and the rare large blue, chalk hill blue and adonis blue), but the others appear later in the year, so a blue one now is likely to be the holly blue butterfly. Look for holly blues in parks and gardens fluttering around the flower beds and, in particular, holly bushes, but bear in mind that this is a species that has booms and busts in terms of population: some years you'll see loads, and other years none at all.

Another early butterfly to emerge is the **speckled wood** – the only butterfly in the UK which can spend the winter either as a caterpillar (which then pupates in spring) or a pupa, ready to bust out as a butterfly on a warm day. Unlike most butterflies, speckled woods aren't reliant on nectar but drink honeydew, the sticky substance excreted by aphids, and this helps them get going when there aren't many wildflowers out yet. These spotty brown butterflies can be found in the dappled shade of woodlands or hedgerows, and the males are extremely territorial. You might see them locked in spiralling aerial battles, seeing off the competition, like boozed-up lads outside a pub. They've recently expanded their range northward, recolonising parts of the north of England and Scotland too.

As we learnt last month, as insect numbers increase in spring, so do numbers of the creatures that eat them, including all the insect-eating birds that come here for the summer to breed. Towards the end of this month, birds like **swallows**, flycatchers (pied and spotted) and **nightingales** begin to return to our shores, which means you might start seeing people mention them – but the unforgettable, otherworldly song of the nightingale can most reliably be heard in the first half of May, largely in the southern and eastern counties. If you'd like to hear one, now's the time to look ahead and start planning a trip to a Wildlife Trust or RSPB site next month, or booking yourself on to a guided walk. But closer to home, do keep listening out for the blackbird whose cheerful, warbling song we learnt last month, especially in mid- to late afternoon: you'll really miss him when he stops singing in three months' time.

Another bird that returns to our shores this month is the enormous, long-legged, beak-clacking white stork. These huge migratory omnivores were once native to Britain, but became extinct 600 years ago. However, a reintroduction programme centred on the rewilded Knepp Estate in West Sussex has proved a great success, and white storks are now breeding there and in a couple of other locations. It's well worth a trip to Knepp to see their huge, messy, treetop nests; you can book guided safaris for the full experience (once intensively farmed, this amazing, hope-filled site now has nightingales, turtle doves, purple emperor butterflies, free-ranging cattle, pig and deer herds and so much more) but a network of public footpaths also means that anyone can visit, for free.

If you live near house sparrows they'll start being really loud now. They live in gangs and there's always a lot of cheeping and chirping, as well as the hysterical balls of feathers euphemistically known as '**sparrow weddings**': usually several males around a single female, and not very romantic at all. But while they might seem ubiquitous if you have them, sparrow numbers have fallen fast across Europe in recent years. The reasons for this are thought to be complex, and research is under way to find out how we can help.

When I was a kid, if you drove somewhere in spring or summer the car's headlights would be covered in dead bugs when you got home. Now, they stay relatively clean – and I find that utterly chilling. Invertebrates form the base of the 'trophic pyramid': imagine a triangle with a base formed mainly of plants, and above it, small creatures like insects, which in turn feed birds and amphibians, which go on to feed the next level up, with apex predators at the top. We're losing that invertebrate layer, and the effects are rippling up the entire food chain: another reason not to use insecticides, and to rewild our parks and gardens wherever we can.

At the end of April, cities across the world take part in the **City Nature Challenge**: check online to see if yours is one of them. Using the iNaturalist app (see Resources), participants take photos of plants, insects and other living things in their local area and submit them to the project, then, in the following week, they're identified and counted. The results are used to help researchers understand urban environments and how we can best coexist with nature.

Each day, note down the very best thing you experienced in the natural world.

Date

Date

Date

Date

Date

Date

First dandelion clock Date: _____   Active seven-spot ladybird

BIRD BY EAR

They arrived last month, but by April you'll definitely have a chiffchaff singing somewhere near you. Once you get your ear in, you'll hear it everywhere: a rhythmical, persistent, somewhat mindless '*dink – dink – dink – dink – dink – dink – dink*' from anywhere with tree cover: city parks, suburban woodlands, canal banks, bits of scrub. Listen to one online or on your Merlin app and compare it to the song of a great tit: can you hear how the great tit usually sings two notes, which go up/down, up/down, like someone saying 'teacher, teacher'? The chiffchaff can't even manage that degree of variation: just
'*dink – dink – dink – dink – dink*'

☐ *Swallows flying overhead* Date: _____   ☐ *Carpet of English bluebells*

Keep a dog poo bag or sandwich bag in your coat pocket: it can be really useful when it comes to taking things home to look at, such as owl pellets or dead insects. It's also great for picking up litter!

Cheerful, beautiful dandelions

🔍 ☐ *Holly blue butterfly* ☐ *Goosegrass* ☐ *The sound of a lawnmower*

Date

Date

Date

Date

Date

Date

☐ *Stinging nettles growing strongly*   ☐ *Cowslips*   ☐ *Garlic mustard*

Date

Date

Date

Date

Date

Date

🔍 ☐ *Speedwell*　☐ *Herb robert (give it a sniff!)*　☐ *Red mason bee*

Seven-spot ladybird on alkanet

Curious about what goes on in your garden after dark? Set up a trailcam and find out! NatureSpy.org is a non-profit wildlife camera retailer that ploughs money back into conservation. Choose ones that run on rechargeable batteries if you can.

☐ *Cows returning to farmland fields*   ☐ *Magnolia tree in flower*

Chiffchaffs are easy to spot while the leaves are still small

When walking at night, wear darker-coloured clothing, leave the dog at home and try not to use a torch if you're hoping to spot wildlife: your eyes will adjust if you give them time. Nights with a good moon are best.

☐ *A street of cherry blossom*   ☐ *Speckled wood butterfly*

Date

Date

Date

Date

Date

Date

☐ *Sparrow 'wedding'*

Date

Date

Date

April is peak cherry blossom viewing time

🔍 *BONUS* ☐ *Baby rabbits* ☐ *Took part in the City Nature Challenge*

Date

Date

Date

*Use all your senses. Look up when birds fall silent:
a bird of prey may be passing overhead. Feel which
way the wind is blowing: it can take your scent
away from wildlife. Touch plants to learn which
are sticky and which are hairy. The sharp smell
of fox can be a clue to the location of their dens.*

☐ *Planned a nightingale walk for next month*　　☐ *Planted sweet peas*

May

*Lushness, plenty and
sheer intoxication;
flowers and sap and
good green growth*

Some people have a favourite month: for me, it's May, particularly the second half. So important is it to me that in recent years I've made it a rule not to travel anywhere where the glorious uprush of this month can't be experienced, if at all possible: so no city breaks, work trips or beach holidays; nothing that will mean I miss a single second of the joyful feeling that rises up in me and makes me exclaim to anyone who'll listen, 'I cannot *believe* I get to be alive on this planet right now and see all this!' After all, who knows how many Mays I might have left?

Because make no mistake, May is a *madness*. Opening with the ancient Gaelic festival of Beltane, now known as May Day, across most of the UK, the soil has warmed up and the risk of night-time frosts has passed or is passing, so the sheer rate of growth – especially if rainfall levels have been decent – is astonishing: at some point this month, go back and look at that little bit of weedy verge you looked at in March. I bet it's utterly transformed.

This month grass turns thick and lush and surges upwards, here and there carpeted – if permitted by gardeners – with **buttercups** and studded with daisies and dandelion clocks; stands of nettles become juicy forests; goosegrass against a sunny fence soon tops my height of 5ft 2in; the little white stars of **greater stitchwort** glow like scattered stars on field edges, and here and there on farmland, **ox-eye daisies** and the first red **poppies** can be seen: these will be at their best next month, and should continue flowering until August. **Comfrey, honesty**[1] and **alkanet** will be busy with bees and, best of all, the **cow parsley** in parks and on roadside verges

---

1 If you find some honesty in bloom, make a note of where it is. We'll be returning to it later in the year.

foams into lacey white froth. Man alive, I *love* cow parsley: feed it into my veins. Sure, it can be a bully that thrives on nitrogen from car exhausts and uses it like kryptonite to outcompete other wildflowers, but in May, I don't care. The way it edges roads in lace and glows in the shadows under trees is glorious, fleeting and extremely photogenic. It never fails to take my breath away.

Less wild but no less beautiful, **lilac** and **wisteria** are both spectacular things to look for this month: wisteria swagging house fronts in waterfalls of pale violet blossom and lilac's heavily scented blooms dangling over garden walls in shades of white, purple and pink. Find your nearest one and inhale it every time you pass. Wisteria, being super-photogenic, has a particular buzz about it on social media, so if you can't find any houses with it near you, follow #wisteria or #wisteriahysteria to join in.

If you live in, or find yourself passing through, the countryside, look out for short-lived, bright yellow fields in squares and parallelograms: this is **rapeseed**, a crop related to mustard that's grown to make cooking oil, animal food and for biofuel. Oh, and don't forget to keep your sweet pea seedlings well-watered, if you planted any – and by 'well-watered' I mean every couple of days, or daily if the weather is hot and dry.

And then, of course, there's the **hawthorn**, which foams along hedges in town and countryside alike. Also known as 'may blossom' for the month in which its flowers peak, hawthorn is, like the blackthorn we met earlier in the year, a classic hedge species, originally planted for its dense growth and sharp thorns which help keep animals from straying. Unlike its earlier-flowering cousin, hawthorn's leaves appear first, and then, in late spring, its densely packed flowers in clotted cream, sometimes grubby pink. Some love its very particular fragrance, while others hate it – and given that the scent contains trace amounts of a chemical called trimethylamine, also released by decaying meat, that's understandable. However, I'm in the former camp: I adore it, if only for its positive associations. It makes me think of springtime, and sunshine, and pure happiness.

I'm writing this during an astonishing year for hawthorn, and my socials are full of gobsmacked people's photos of trees and hedges so heavy with creamy blossom they droop; there's debate, too, about whether it's related to last year's drought, a way to make up for not having been able to produce many berries in the previous year. You may have realised this already, but I *love* the collective aspect of nature noticing, particularly in the age of social media. It feels like being part of something: a wave of joy and excitement that sweeps through the country with each passing month. And it costs absolutely nothing to join in.

This is the month when all the big trees like oaks, ashes, planes and sycamores clothe themselves in foliage. Each year the timings vary a little, and are worth noting and comparing; each spot also differs from the next and sometimes, one oak will come into leaf a week before its neighbour, just yards away. By the end of the month, though, the last of the bare branches we've been looking at for months will be hidden by green.

In parks, streets and village greens, **horse chestnuts** – conker trees – also put out their spectacular, upright flower heads in either cream or, less commonly, dark pink. These short-lived blooms can cover a big, healthy horse chestnut like candles on a green cloud, but peer closely, for each individual flower is the betrayer of its own dirty secret: they start off pure ivory, but once pollinated – usually by an early bee – a tiny crimson stain appears. Meanwhile, female **poplar trees** release their seeds, each one surrounded by flossy white fluff that helps the wind distribute them, and this can lie so thickly on the ground it almost looks like snow.

In May, the **dawn chorus** reaches its peak with International Dawn Chorus Day on the first Sunday of the month. If you've never heard the dawn chorus, now's the time: it really is something, and by July it'll all be over, as breeding season ends and some of our avian visitors depart for sunnier climes. Check the sunrise time and aim to be somewhere green and bushy half an hour before then, so you can hear the first few notes swell into a breathtaking chorus as the light rises, then fall away into the normal background birdsong of a warm spring day. I do it at least once, every May, and I never regret it. And then I go back to bed.

So why now? Spring is when many birds are seeking a mate and then defending a territory in which to find food, so they can breed successfully; singing is a way of doing both, and carries much further at dawn, when there's less background noise. By May, our year-round species like robins and wrens have been joined by a cohort of summer visitors, some of which we met earlier in the year, here to raise chicks and take advantage of a spike in food availability. Many of these migrants – blackcaps and whitethroats, for example, but also celebrated but fast-declining species like **cuckoos** and nightingales – are strong singers, adding to the levels of spring song at both sunup and sundown.

The first part of May is your best window for hearing a **nightingale**, if you'd like to. Only about 5,500 pairs of these magical birds return to our shores now, mostly to the southern and eastern counties: the rewilded Knepp Estate has around forty singing males, but you can also look online for RSPB and Wildlife Trust sites or book on to a special guided walk. They sing in the daytime, too, so it doesn't have to be an after-dark expedition; however, night is when they sound most spectacular, not least because all the other birds have fallen silent. The aim of the nocturnal performances are to attract a mate, so once they've paired they tend to tail off, with few after-dark singers left by the end of the month. For most birds, breeding location and season is timed to coincide with food availability – and not just any food, but the kind that's suitable to feed their young. It's a tricky business, bringing up helpless chicks, not least because to survive they need moisture and that generally rules out dry foods like seeds and insects. So – as I mentioned back in January – many of our most beloved garden birds rely on caterpillars for baby food, as they're soft, moist and easily digestible. The peak season for caterpillars to emerge from eggs needs to coincide with when there are lots of fresh young leaves for them to eat – and that, in turn, means spring. And of course, **birds' eggs** and baby birds are important food for several other creatures, such as **nest-raiding magpies**, stoats and weasels, hedgehogs and even snakes.

However, climate change is disrupting this ancient, complex rhythm, with studies showing that many key spring flowers are blooming a full month earlier in the UK now than they did as recently as the 1980s. Research is ongoing into the knock-on effects of this change on invertebrates, birds and everything else. It may be that some species can adapt (sparrows, for example, can feed their young on aphids as well as, or instead of, caterpillars) – but others may not be able to, as the cycle they have evolved to live within changes too fast for them to keep up.

Among the summer visitors is the bird that lifts my heart when it arrives in May more than any other: the **swift**. They're those black, wheeling shurikens that let out high-pitched screams from clear, blue skies: the true sound of summer to me. When I lived in London I usually saw my first on May 9th; now, in Suffolk, it's around May 5th, though some people spot their first a few days earlier, or even, if the weather's warm and the wind is helping them get here, at the very end of April. They're only in the UK for eight weeks or so – they'll usually start heading off around the end of July, beginning of August – so the time we get to spend with them is precious. And once you learn how miraculous they are, I promise you'll be as elated by spotting your first swift each year as I am – and as thousands of other people are across the UK, too. Follow some bird lovers and swift hashtags on your socials and watch your feed explode with excitement in the first week of May, as our swifts make landfall again.

These birds are *literally* out of this world: they live in the air as fish live in the ocean – eating, drinking, mating and sleeping on the wing. They only ever land in order to raise chicks, and even then, not on the ground: they nest in crevices and cavities on tall buildings, from which they drop back out into the waiting air. Each year, the new chicks fledge and soon set off on a journey of 4,000 miles to their wintering grounds in Africa, and get this: they won't land again until they've reached sexual maturity and have mated (on the wing) for the first time, which can be four years later. That's *four years* spent in continuous flight: scooping up flies, mosquitoes, windblown spiders and other aerial plankton in their wide gapes like tiny, feathered basking sharks; drinking falling raindrops; spiralling up to nap on warm thermals at dusk and dawn.

Every year fewer swifts breed here – they've declined by 60 per cent since 1995 – and in 2021 they were added to the UK's Red List of birds of conservation concern. Part of the reason is that modern buildings tend to have fewer holes and crevices for them to nest in, and some people even put up mesh or block them up. If you can, consider putting up a swift box, or join a local swift group who help make sure there are nesting places for them to return to each May.

When I lived in London there was a small colony in a block of flats near my house. One spring, scaffolding was put up, draped with netting, while some repair work was done. By April it had been completed but the netting remained. I got the number of the contractor from a sign on the scaffolding and started making friendly phone calls, and it was taken down just in time for the swifts to return. I cannot even tell you how much joy I felt, seeing them arrive back, having flown all the way from Africa, and zoom into their old nesting places. Making a small difference like this is relatively easy and unbelievably rewarding, so I'd urge you to look out for your local swifts (and other non-human neighbours) however you can.

Another problem for migratory insect-eaters like swifts, swallows, house martins, flycatchers and many others, is a steep drop in insect abundance over the last half-century. This collapse in numbers is happening eight times faster than that of birds or mammals, with one study, published in the journal *Biological Conservation*,[2] showing that at the current rate of decline they could be all but gone within a century. Given invertebrates' roles as food for other creatures, pollinators of plants and decomposers of organic matter, that would threaten life on Earth. So, we urgently need to build back our bug numbers, and protect the ones we have left. Now, when I find myself batting craneflies away from my face on a walk or picking unknown insects out of my teeth when I'm cycling, I feel elated: think of all that food for birds and other critters to feast on! When you're outdoors in spring and summer,

---

2 'Worldwide Decline of the Entomofauna', by Francisco Sánchez-Bayo and Kris A. G. Wyckhuys, School of Life & Environmental Sciences, The University of Sydney (2019)

get into the habit of looking around and asking yourself: where are all the insects? And how can I help to get them back?

One of the key species I look out for in May is called **St Mark's fly** because it was once thought to first emerge on St Mark's Day, April 25th. Also known as the hawthorn fly, it's jet black, ambles about in the air in an aimless sort of way and has long, dangly legs that visibly hang down. Another is the aptly named **mayfly**, which hatches from water – sometimes in sparkling, sunlit clouds – and only lives a day. Neither of these insects bite or sting, and both are incredibly important food sources for swifts, swallows, house martins and other birds.

Earlier in the year we met some of the first butterflies to be seen on the wing: species that are able to spend the winter as adults, ready to get going as the weather warms up. In May we see the first of the year's new butterflies to emerge from chrysalises, and the **orange-tip butterfly** (the male of which looks exactly as you'd imagine) usually kicks things off. Its caterpillars need cuckoo flowers and garlic mustard to eat, so if you have either local to you, protect them and grow more, if you can.

Butterflies get all the good press, but moths are more numerous, more interesting (to me, anyway) and are crucial pollinators of many plant species as well as food for lots of other living things. A fascinating spectacle you might spot in May is hedges or bushes completely shrouded in what looks like cobwebs. The emerging caterpillars of a couple of types of ermine moth are the weavers, and the silken sheets are there to protect the vulnerable larvae from being eaten. **Ermine caterpillar webs** may look startling, but they're harmless and tend to disappear naturally, without damaging the vegetation.

Also harmless but startling is our final species to spot this month, the aptly named **maybug,** or – if you really must – cockchafer. Whirring around like clumsy steampunk battlebots at dusk and during the night, these huge brown flying insects spend around four years underground as larvae before emerging as short-lived adults to mate. Like many of our insects they used to be much more common, and today are easier to find in the south of the UK. They don't bite or sting and are loved by owls and bigger bats like noctules.

Each day, note down the very best thing you experienced in the natural world.

Date

Date

Date

Date

Date

Date

🔍 ☐ *First swift* Date: _____   ☐ *Orange-tip butterfly* Date: _____

BIRD BY EAR

Just as, in early spring, a part of my brain is always
listening out for a blackbird, so in May I am
subconsciously tuned to the frequency of swifts.
Their extremely high-pitched, drawn-out screams
from far overhead are impossible to confuse with
any other bird vocalisation, and are likely to be a
sound you're already familiar with from back-garden
barbecues, lazy afternoons in parks and holidays to
hot European destinations. All you need to do is to
tell your brain that when you hear that thin scream,
it's important: look up! Look up! Look up!

☐ *Horse chestnut flowers*　　☐ *Poppies*　　☐ *Hawthorn blossom*

Make sure you get up early at least once in May to hear the dawn chorus swell, reach its spectacular peak, and fade away. You can always go back to bed afterwards!

Cow parsley, poppies and goosegrass: a May bouquet

 ☐ *Clouds of cow parsley*   ☐ *Greater stitchwort*   ☐ *Bees on comfrey*

Date

Date

Date

Date

Date

Date

☐ *Alkanet in flower*   ☐ *A carpet of buttercups*   ☐ *Yellow fields of rapeseed*

Date

Date

Date

Date

Date

Date

🔍 ☐ *Swags of wisteria*   ☐ *Sweet-smelling lilac*   ☐ *St Mark's flies*

Left to right: a swallow, a swift and a house martin

Be patient when learning to recognise birdsong. It takes practice to tune your ear in and teach it to distinguish between one sound and another, but it will happen. Keep listening!

☐ *A magpie causing a commotion*   ☐ *The dawn chorus*   ☐ *Poplar tree fluff*

Magpies are natural nest predators, as this great tit knows

If you like your garden to look neat and perfect,
take a moment to wonder why. Nature thrives
under a relaxed regime: can you let a little tangle
and untidiness in, knowing you're adding to
the richness of your entire neighbourhood?

☐ *Ermine caterpillar webs*   ☐ *Honesty in bloom*

Date

Date

Date

Date

Date

Date

☐ *Maybug in flight* ☐ *Ox-eye daisy* ☐ *Empty wild bird's egg*

Date

Date

Date

An orange-tip on garlic mustard; a passing St Mark's fly

🔍 *BONUS* ☐ *Cuckoo calling* ☐ *Nightingale in song*

Date

Date

Date

Date

> *To recover the skeleton of a small dead creature,
> pop it in the foot of some old tights and tie a
> knot. Bury it in a damp spot with a stone on top
> and leave for a couple of months. Dig up and
> rinse. A little extremely diluted bleach can help
> whiten the bones, but don't go overboard.*

☐ *A cloud of mayflies over water*

June

Roses and elderflowers and
tall grass topped with seed
heads; swifts and swallows
carve the blue skies overhead

First off, what kind of spring has it been so far? In your part of the British Isles, has it been colder than usual or wetter; or has it been sunny and dry? How do you think your nearby nature has fared, given the weather – well, or not so good? The Met Office publishes seasonal assessments at the end of each quarter; they're buried deep on its website but if you search 'Met Office spring 2025', for example, you can read a summary of the season and start getting a feel for the bigger picture and how your area fits in to it.

We're fast coming up to the longest day of the year, on or around June 21st, which means summer is truly upon us. The days are really long now, the noon sun getting ever higher in the sky, which means lots of energy for plant growth. And with so many plants in bloom and so many insects about it's a good time for citizen science and pro-nature projects, one of the biggest of which is **30 Days Wild**, organised by The Wildlife Trusts. The challenge is to do one wild thing each day for the whole month, and it's a lot of fun, particularly for kids. You can find more information online. It's also the month of The Great Yorkshire Creature Count, Insect Week (organised by the Royal Entomological Society) and Churches Count on Nature, when volunteers come together to survey the wildlife in churchyards, cemeteries and burial grounds across the UK. That may seem niche, but because graveyards usually haven't had any chemical treatments such as agricultural pesticides or fertilisers, they can be incredibly important places for rare and threatened species.

To me, June is mainly about grass: it's the month when farmers in the south of the UK usually begin to cut their meadows to make fodder for animals over the winter, sending the sweet smell of cut grass into the warm air. The grass is either formed into dry bales, in which case it's called hay, or wrapped in plastic to help it ferment: this is known as haylage or silage, depending on the moisture content. Haymaking generally starts before harvest-time, which is when cereal crops, legumes and other field crops are brought in, but in some years and in some places, it will start later than June, and the two may even overlap or coincide.

Towards the end of the month, once it has set seed, you'll see standing grass starting to look dry and tired; if it's cut, and there's rain, it'll soon green up and start growing again, and depending on the weather there might be a second hay cut later in the year. Grass's close cousins, the cereal crops, are also beginning to ripen: both wheat and barley will be forming ears, depending on weather conditions and when they were sown, but they won't be fully ripe and ready for harvest for several weeks.

I grew up just thinking of grass as just the green stuff lawns and sports pitches was carpeted in, that was mown close and low. But there are around 160 species of grass in Britain and Ireland, and if it's allowed to grow tall and set seed, as in a hay meadow or the wild areas of a park, you'll be able to see how the various types differ, by looking at their seed heads: it's like a big crowd at Glastonbury when everyone waves their banners and flags. And I love the names for grasses: from **Yorkshire fog**, with its purplish pennants, to cocksfoot, red fescue, quaking grass, false-brome, common bent and timothy.

Tall, species-diverse grass should be busy with craneflies, spiders, moths and other insects, though moths have declined steeply in recent years and it's rare to walk through long grass and see clouds of them billowing up from their daytime resting places as you commonly would have seen fifty years ago. You might see **meadow brown** and **skipper butterflies** (both large and small varieties) in grassy areas, but there's often a bit of a dip in butterfly numbers in June as the spring-flying species we met earlier in the year, like brimstones, commas, cabbage whites, holly blues and peacocks, die off, having mated and laid eggs; it's usually around now that I see my final orange-tip of the season, too. However, more butterflies will emerge next month, and by the time of the Big Butterfly Count there should be lots on the wing again.

In June, grasshoppers and crickets are in the process of completing their metamorphosis deep amid unmown grass: they go through several 'instars' as they grow from eggs to nymphs to adulthood, at which point you'll hear them starting to sing by rubbing their back legs together (more on that next month). Here and there little blobs of **cuckoo spit** protect growing froghoppers, tiny plant-eating insects with a powerful jump. The froth is formed when they fart plant sap they've eaten out of their bums to create protective bubble wrap to live in, and it's completely harmless – but that didn't stop several UK tabloids running scare stories about it in 2023. For some reason, our media seems bent on telling us to be frightened of the natural world. These stories would be funny if they didn't have the potential to be so damaging at a time when we all need to lean in to nature, not away from it, and I suggest the next time you see such a story you contact the editor and kick off. That's what I did, along with many others, and the cuckoo spit non-story was quickly amended. A small triumph, but it beggars belief that someone wrote it at all.

Dragonflies, which begin their lives underwater, emerge to become fast-flying aerial predators of flies and other insects. When they're ready, the larvae crawl out of the water and shuck off their skins; these fragile and minutely detailed empty shells, or **exuviae**, remain on rushes and other bankside vegetation and are pretty easy to find. I think they're absolutely fascinating, and used to collect them as a kid. Most amazingly, each dragonfly's four large wings unfold from tiny packets, which can be seen on each shell and look rather like a little backpack.

In the southern and central regions of the UK, **hornets** are on the wing in June, too, looking like much larger, more golden versions of wasps. People often freak out when they see one, because of their size, but they're gentle giants and just want to go about their business. I love seeing these majestic creatures: they're an indication that there's lots of insects for them to eat further down the trophic pyramid, and that's always a good sign.

June's sunshine means that loads of native wildflowers are at their best now: **field bindweed** decorates grassy bits of waste ground with tiny pink-and-white striped circus tops, tall spires of **foxgloves** nod in the breeze and are abuzz with **bumblebees**, **brambles** put out their dirty pink flowers in promise of blackberries to come, while in the countryside, ox-eye daisies look gorgeous along field edges, especially when mixed with red poppies and blue **cornflowers**, all of which will bloom right through summer.

Colonising the dry, compacted soil along the sides of paths, where few other things can grow, you'll often see one of my favourite wild plants to introduce people to. Its leaves are green and feathery, and its small blooms are yellow, dome-shaped and completely lacking in petals. It's not spectacular, but it's a lot of fun: pick a bit and crush it between your fingers. Not only does it look like a tiny pineapple, but it smells like one, too! You've just met the rather obviously-named **pineapple weed**, a member of the

mayweed family which arrived here from North America in the late 1800s and spread quickly as its seeds were the perfect shape and size to be distributed by early, rubber car tyres driving on dirt roads. I'm willing to bet that's one wildflower whose name you won't forget.

Even **stinging nettles** come into modest flower in June, and will continue flowering all summer: look for odd little nothingy-coloured tassels dangling off their tops. Nettles may not be top of your list of wild plants to love, but they're one of our most important species for wildlife: as well as being the food plant for over forty species of insect, the aphids that live on them are eaten by both ladybirds and birds such as sparrows, while seed-eating birds like chaffinches, sparrows and siskins eat its seeds when they ripen in autumn. More and more people are coming to understand this now, and are leaving nettles to grow where they can instead of getting rid of them. It's a really positive step.

But in terms of flowers, June belongs to **elderflowers** and **roses**: both the big, blowsy types you see growing in gardens or climbing up house fronts, and the **dog rose**, their wild ancestor, with its simple, five-petalled flower in shades of white and pink, garlanding the hedgerows on long, arching stems. Later – unless the hedge is cut back – each dog rose will become a rose hip, as in 'hips and haws' (haws are the fruits of hawthorns). Incredibly high in vitamin C, during the Second World War people were paid by the government to collect hips; these were boiled down, strained and combined with sugar to make a syrup to stop children becoming vitamin-deficient as food shortages bit.

Elderflowers can also be harvested, in their case to make delicious cordial, liqueur or champagne; making cordial is relatively easy and you can find recipes online. Look for large, creamy, fragrant plates made up of hundreds of tiny florets set against dark foliage, held up to the June sunshine and nodding in the breeze. Closer to home, if you planted **sweet pea** seedlings and kept them well-watered they should start to produce flowers in the second half of this month. Make sure you pick them and bring them inside to enjoy the gorgeous fragrance; picking every couple of days encourages each plant to keep making more. If you don't, it'll set seed and think its job of reproduction is done, and it can retire!

All these flowers mean that June is boom time for pollinators, including hoverflies – some of which are migrants and arrive here in vast numbers, enough to be seen on radar – as well the more familiar honeybees. On really warm, sunny days you may even see (or hear!) a **honeybee swarm**, as a colony of bees set out in search of a new hive. These usually occur in June and July between 11am and 4pm, when the sun is high and warm in the sky, and can begin as a loose cloud of bees that settle quickly into a sort of clump, on a branch or other structure. This is a natural process and very exciting to watch, from a distance. The best thing to do is leave them to it. If they're in your garden, though, you might want to call a local beekeeper who may be able to come and take them away; search online or via the British Beekeepers Association.

I've seen two bee swarms and both times I heard them before I saw them – a reminder that contact with nature comes via all our senses, and the more you tune in to sounds the more you'll be able to filter out what's 'normal' for a particular place and time, and thus get alerted to unusual and interesting things you might otherwise miss. Another audio example is the kingfisher, which usually utters an incredibly high-pitched '*peep*!' while flying upriver. Lots of my kingfisher sightings have happened because I've heard that sound and managed to whip my head around in time.

If you live in an area of the country that's home to **stag beetles** (south-east England, in particular London; also parts of the south-west coast and Severn Valley), keep an eye open for them this month, especially at twilight. At up to 7.5cm, with their huge antler-like mandibles, the males are unmistakable; the females are much smaller at 3–4cm, but are still a substantial insect. Completely harmless (the males' mandibles are for battling rivals), these spectacular beings spend several years as a fat grub living on rotting wood; their life as an adult beetle is short, its only purpose to reproduce. I grew up in Surrey and used to delight in seeing them every summer; now I live in Suffolk, where they're much, much rarer, and I miss them. Globally threatened, they need our help, so if you spot one this month or next, do search online for 'PTES stag beetle count' and report your sighting.

In June, gardens, parks, woods and hedgerows are full of **baby birds**, and you'll hear their faint, wheezy calls absolutely everywhere. Stop and wait quietly and you'll often be able to see them perched somewhere, all fluffy and wobbly, their beaks still looking too big for their heads and their parents still bringing them food. For some species, once they've raised a brood successfully, breeding season is over; others, including blackbirds, robins and wrens, will go on to have a second and, depending on the weather conditions, even try for a third.

As some species finish breeding, the volume of song starts to decrease, something you'll notice if you listen to the dawn chorus again this month. By the end of July things will seem really quiet, so enjoy all the birdsong while you can – in particular your local blackbird, who will still be in good voice. Have you learnt to tell him apart from his competitors yet?

House sparrows will have two to three broods and in a good year will sometimes lay for a fourth time. Although house sparrows are widespread, they're also on the Red

List in the UK, meaning they are a bird of conservation concern. This is due to the speed at which their numbers are falling, so each nest site and each brood is now important. Ignoring the special sparrow terrace I installed for them, 'my' sparrows nest in my swift box, and in June my front garden comes alive with their ridiculous, chirpy, clumsy chicks, picking aphids off my flowers, getting into squabbles and bouncing around all over the place like total idiots. I love them so much.

One final thing: don't let the **summer solstice** – the longest day and shortest night – pass you by. We know from prehistoric structures like Stonehenge how hugely important it was for our ancestors to mark the solstices, and I think ritual can and should be just as important to us today.[1] Doing things that are meaningful to us at the key points of the year can help us make powerful and lasting connections to the cycle of the seasons, not to mention being a deeply atavistic, nature-connected enactment of our shared cultural memory. Have a think about what would be meaningful for you, whether domestic or dramatic, alone or communal. There's no right or wrong; what does your heart say the summer solstice means?

I usually go for a **night walk** to make the most of the long, light evening on its slow journey to night. I love being out as dusk falls and the daytime creatures clock off, to be replaced by the night shift. Many of my most memorable natural encounters, from the evening chorus to hunting barn owls and barking deer, have happened as night begins to fall. Put on some insect repellent, wear darker coloured clothes (consider reflective straps if you'll be walking on roads), take

---

1 *Slow Seasons: A Creative Guide to Reconnecting with Nature the Celtic Way* by Rosie Steer is a lovely guide to incorporating ancient rituals, traditions and ceremonies into our modern lives.

a torch but try not to use it,[2] and leave the dog at home. Even if you don't see any wildlife, being out while everyone else is slumped in front of the telly feels really special and can connect you to all the previous generations who lived in a world without artificial light, and were familiar with sunset, and darkness, and our age-old companions: the vast, eternal panoply of stars.

My friend, the writer Josie George (@porridgebrain) picks and presses flowers from her garden at midsummer so she can look at them again in the depths of winter and remind herself of what's to come. But whether it's a wild swim, an evening picnic, dancing all night or just picking a posy of flowers, take time to make your own embodied and emotional connection with the glorious midpoint of the year.

---

2 It takes about 20 minutes for the rod cells in your retinas to begin producing a photopigment called rhodopsin that allows you to see in dim light. If, during that process, you look at a bright light source, the rhodopsin decomposes, and you have to start again.

Each day, note down the very best thing you experienced in the natural world.

Date

Date

Date

Date

Date

Date

🔍 ☐ **First sweet peas** Date: _____   ☐ **Skipper butterfly** Date: _____

BIRD BY EAR

This month I'd like to introduce you to the relatively
tuneless (but extremely persistent) cheeping and
chirping of our friend and close neighbour: the
house sparrow. Each tweet is slightly modulated
and chirrupy, rather than the robotic notes of the
chiffchaff, and the time intervals are less regular,
though the courtship song consists of a male going
'*CHOYP? CHOYP? CHOYP? CHOYP?*' seemingly
forever. Females make a chittering noise, either to
greet males or to chase off other females; the other
giveaway is that you'll rarely hear a single sparrow
as they're so sociable. Generally, you'll hear a whole
gang of them making a racket.

☐ *Meadow brown butterfly* Date: _____   ☐ *Marked the summer solstice*

Mark midsummer, midwinter and the spring and autumn equinoxes with a ritual of your own. It can be as simple as picking flowers or as dramatic as dancing around a bonfire: choose your own way of making meaning from the turning points of the year.

June's bounty: dog roses and elderflowers

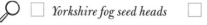 Yorkshire fog seed heads   ☐ Field bindweed   ☐ Bramble flowers

Date

Date

Date

Date

Date

Date

☐ *Bumblebees in foxgloves*   ☐ *Dragonfly exuviae*

Date

Date

Date

Date

Date

Date

🔍 ☐ *Elderflowers*   ☐ *Cuckoo spit*   ☐ *Nettles in flower*

Find out about farmland. If you have some near you, or somewhere you plan to visit, check the farm's website for visiting days when you can find out what they're doing for wildlife. LEAF (Linking Environment and Farming) organises an Open Farm Sunday, usually in June: farmsunday.org/visit-a-farm

Glorious grasses and a beautiful meadow brown

☐ *Pineapple weed (smell it!)*   ☐ *Dog roses*

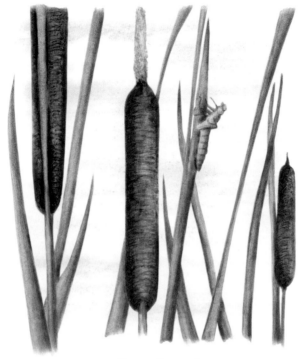

Dragonfly exuvia

Carnivore poo is often long and pointed at one end,
whereas herbivore poo is often small and cylindrical.
All animal droppings may change colour depending
on the time of year and what's been on the menu.

  Garden roses  Cornflowers A hornet

Date

Date

Date

Date

Date

Date

☐ *Wheezing baby birds*   ☐ *Went for a night walk*

Date

Date

Date

Sparrow chicks: so demanding!

🔍 *BONUS* ☐ *Spotted a honeybee swarm* ☐ *Completed 30 Days Wild*

Date

Date

Date

*Make sure you clean your bird feeders regularly
to prevent the spread of trichomonosis, a
terrible disease that affects several bird
species, most commonly finches.*

☐ *Made elderflower cordial*   ☐ *Stag beetle – male or female*

July

*High summer, when tall grass
fades to golden thatch. Insects
abound, by day and night*

Before we begin: are your **tomatoes** ripening yet, and how are your sweet peas? If you planted some in a sunny spot with something to climb up, and kept them well-watered, you should be picking fragrant bunches for your bedside table now. Do make a note of the date you first pick some, if you haven't already, so that next year you can start saying things like, 'Hasn't it been a great year for sweet peas?' or 'It's not been as good for tomatoes this year as last', while shaking your head sadly, which for some reason is extremely satisfying.

But if you didn't manage to plant either tomatoes or sweet peas, or they didn't make it, *do not worry*: the fact that there is always next year, or the one after, is one of the great comforts of living within the cycle of the seasons. In my garden, something dies, gets forgotten about or fails to thrive every year, and every year that follows is an opportunity to try again, which means that I'm always looking forward, always being beckoned on through time by optimism and anticipation. I love that feeling.

Since the solstice, the days have been shortening and the sun hasn't risen quite so high in the sky, but the effect is offset by the capacity of the earth to absorb and then radiate heat. This means that the hottest period of the year usually lags four to six weeks later, in July and early August.

Once it's set seed, any uncut grass dries out and falls down, while in the countryside, cereal crops turn golden. Many of the spring wildflowers are now over, but **hogweed** (a bigger, beefier version of cow parsley) blooms on verges, its white umbels the stage for hunting (and mating) **soldier beetles**.[1]

On waste ground, look carefully at bright yellow **ragwort**, the food plant for over 130 insects and the seventh most important wild plant for pollinators in the UK: you might see the stripy caterpillars of the gorgeous **cinnabar moth** on it.[2] The adult cinnabar moths, in their striking red and black livery, can be seen on the wing during the day at this time of year. The same goes for spectacular **Jersey tiger moths**, which can be seen from around the second week of July in the southern counties of the UK.

In damp ditches and on riverbanks you might see tall stands of pink-and-white flowered **Himalayan balsam**. It might look pretty, but this fast-growing annual hasn't been here long enough for many things to have learnt to eat it or otherwise keep it in check, so it can form vast thickets on waterways that choke out all other wildflowers – including those that feed and support lots of other life. Then, when it dies back in autumn, it leaves swathes of bank exposed to water and at risk of washing away.

A couple of years ago I spotted two stands of Himalayan balsam near my cottage, both in ditches that drain into our local river. Tackling it when in bloom is risky, as the ripe seed pods, which produce vast numbers of seeds, can throw them up to 7m when touched, but I managed to cut the flower heads off very carefully and bag them up. I returned the following year and pulled up each new, shallow-rooted plant

---

1   The UK has several dozen species of soldier beetle, the most well known of which – the common red (which is generally orange) – is known as the 'Hogweed Bonking Beetle' for the ubiquity of its copulating pairs. The name was added to the UK's Invertebrate Site Register in the 1980s, as an entomologists' in-joke; despite its later deletion, it stuck.

2   It's best not to pick ragwort as the sap can blister your skin.

before it could set seed; as the seeds are quite short-lived, I hope to eradicate both stands before any of it makes its way into the river. I tell you this not to toot my own trumpet, but because I was inspired to tackle it after seeing someone else post online about doing the same. You don't have to be an expert, an activist or a conservationist to measurably help nature, and one of the best things you can do, I believe, is share knowledge – so if you do manage to do something helpful, consider yourself encouraged to pass the message on in whatever way you can.

The pretty, magenta flowers of **rosebay willowherb** appear around now and will bloom into September, often on railway cuttings and building sites; in fact, so fond is it of burnt or recently disturbed soil and rubble that it was dubbed 'fireweed' or sometimes 'bombweed' due to its dramatic colonisation of bomb sites during the London Blitz. In grassier areas look out for **knapweed**, a purple-flowered, thistle-like (but not prickly) wildflower that also blooms from June right through to September. Bees, butterflies and moths absolutely adore it, and its seeds are a favourite of birds like goldfinches, which will flock to it in twittering groups, or 'charms'.

Buddleia is another recent coloniser of railway cuttings and waste ground, including cracks in buildings, sometimes quite high up. Originating in stony, mountainous parts of central China and Japan, it was brought here in the 1890s and quickly became naturalised. It is classed by DEFRA as an 'invasive non-native' and is viewed as a serious problem on Britain's railways due to the cost of eradication; it also grows very vigorously and can quickly shade out less robust plants, reducing biodiversity. However, it's absolutely loved by pollinators: not for nothing has it become known as 'the butterfly bush'. I have one in my front garden, and at this time of year, when its flower heads are arching and drooping all over the place like purple fag ash, it's *covered* in butterflies, hoverflies and bees.

My buddleia is busy by night, too: we forget how much pollinating goes on after dark, largely by moths – in fact, new research conducted in Leeds shows that moths perform a third of all pollinating visits, and also pollinate some species that bees can't. The study also found that buddleia pollen was the most common kind found on moths' bodies, underlining the growing importance to nature of this non-native shrub.

So, is buddleia a hero plant or a pernicious invader? As with grey squirrels, cow parsley, wasps or many other creatures, you'll get a different answer depending on who you ask – a reminder that plants and animals, like people, can't usually be sorted into bins marked 'goodies' and 'baddies', no matter how much we prefer the world in black and white. Some garden centres now offer seed-sterile varieties of buddleia such as the yellow-flowered *Buddleia* x *weyeriana* 'Sungold', so if you're thinking of planting one for pollinators, that's what I'd recommend. The smaller Flutterby and Cascade series of cultivars are also sterile, and can be grown in a pot.

Look out, all summer, for the **hummingbird hawk-moth**. This amazing, day-flying creature looks and behaves very like its namesake, hovering in front of tube-shaped flowers such as buddleia, red valerian, nicotiana and honeysuckle, its wings a blur, while it probes for nectar with its long tongue. Incredibly, it can even fly backwards, making it hard to mistake for anything else. Most hummingbird hawk-moths seen in the UK are visitors from southern Europe and North Africa, with some years seeing a huge influx and other years, relatively few. Some do breed here, but so far, they've struggled to survive winter; however, that may soon change. Its cousin the dusk-flying,

pink-and-green elephant hawk-moth is also pretty amazing; we'll be meeting its caterpillar next month.

The **Big Butterfly Count** usually takes place towards the end of July into the start of August: peak season for the UK's butterflies. It takes only 15 minutes, you can do it any time within a roughly three-week period, and anyone, right across the country, can take part. By monitoring the numbers of butterflies and some day-flying moths, scientists can get a really good feel for how nature is faring, as butterflies are considered to be key biodiversity indicators. Plus, it's an excellent excuse to sit outside, or at a window, for quarter of an hour, and just drink in the summer scene. Search online for details of how to take part, or download the app (see Resources). The results are later published on an interactive map. You might also want to check online this month for the dates of **Solitary Bee Week**. It's not a citizen science project but a week of awareness, with activities and information and things to do.

It's now the height of the **dragonfly** season and they can be seen preying on smaller insects above and around water but also quite some distance away. Around 300 million years ago flying insects were massive, with dragonfly-like creatures having wingspans of up to 70cm. It's thought that the reason they could get that big is because oxygen was more concentrated in the air – 30 per cent as opposed to 21 per cent today – allowing them to take in more oxygen for flight via their tracheae: tiny tubes that do the job of lungs. They seem to have shrunk in time with the evolution of birds, when smaller bodies helped them evade being caught;

today, one of their key predators is the **hobby**,[3] a small bird of prey with ginger 'trousers' and long, pointed wings. The hobby arrives in April and leaves in September, and as well as hunting dragonflies, it is fast and agile enough to catch a swift in flight.

Today's less chunky dragonflies can still be pretty impressive, not least for their hunting ability. On a walk one July I spotted some frenzied insect activity on the surface of one of the village lanes near my cottage, and when I got close I saw it was an emperor dragonfly fighting with a wasp. I got my phone out to take a picture, at which point the dragonfly delivered the *coup de grâce* with its jaws and took off, carrying the unfortunate wasp's head. Slightly chillingly, it circled me slowly at eye level before zooming away.

But speaking of swifts: they'll be gone very soon, so do pay attention to those wheeling sickles, those high-pitched calls and the 'screaming parties' you might see blasting low over the streets like formations of jet fighters – a good indication that there is a nest nearby. Swifts start leaving for Africa around the middle of the month, depending on the weather conditions, and by early August they'll usually be on their way – only to return again, after our insects, around the beginning of May next year.

Long grass in sunny spots should be abuzz with **grasshoppers** by now. As a (very) rough guide, grasshoppers zither by day (the technical term is 'stridulate') while **crickets**, which have longer antennae, tune up at dusk. Both insects use their bodies as instruments, the grasshopper by rubbing its back legs against its wing casings, the cricket by rubbing its wings together. And both can jump long

---

3   Fun fact: when Peter Adolph invented a tabletop football game, his initial name for it – 'hobby' – was rejected for being too generic. So he called it 'Subbuteo' instead, from the hobby bird's Latin name of *Falco subbuteo*.

distances; I used to *love* trying to catch them (gently) when I was a child. On the rare occasions that I was successful, the feeling of it in my hand, using all the strength in those big back legs to try and push my fingers open, was unforgettable: a little clockwork being made of compressed muscle and intention and two brass springs.

There are twenty-seven native species of grasshopper and cricket in the UK, and more which have made this country their home. They're crucial links in the food chain, munched on by birds, small mammals and even some spiders, and crickets also do a great job of controlling aphids. If you're able to leave some areas of grass in your garden to grow tall, you could help these springy singers thrive.

There's no way to tell you when your local '**flying ant day**' will be: it varies from place to place and year to year, it can recur several times and there isn't one day across the country, more like 'flying ant season'. However, you could well experience a flight day this month or next: it usually happens during a period of hot and humid weather, when there isn't much of a breeze.

Common black ants are the species most observed in flying ant surveys, although other kinds of ant do the same thing. They form complex underground colonies in warm, sunny ground in cities and countryside. When the colony reaches a certain size, newly hatched queens and males will take flight and seek each other out; each queen will usually mate with several of the smaller males. Once that's accomplished, the males quickly die off, whereas each queen will land, chew off her own wings (hardcore) and look for a good spot to start a new colony, using the sperm she's gathered inside her. She'll be able to lay eggs for the rest of her life without mating again, and that life could last for an astonishing fifteen years.

Now, cards on the table: I have an aversion to creatures in swarms, whether it's bees, ants or spider crabs. But despite my discomfort, I know that flying ant season is a healthy and crucially important part of the natural cycle: all you have to do is look up and see swifts, swallows, house martins and even gulls absolutely feasting on them to know that. What's more, ant colonies are good soil improvers. Sometimes, our feelings about nature – however uncomfortable – aren't the best guide to what's good.

I often start to see the first **arum berries** this month. We met lords-and-ladies back in February, when its rolled leaves started to appear in shady places, followed by a white, lily-like flower; from about now onwards, a spike of orangey-red berries will appear. They're poisonous, but that's no cause for a tabloid panic. Lots of common plants that we live in close proximity to are poisonous, including yew, bluebells, foxgloves, tulips, hemlock and lily-of-the-valley, and they cause absolutely no harm, while being vital parts of our ecosystems or gardens. The sensible question to ask isn't, 'Is it poisonous?' but 'How often is someone harmed?' The answer is likely to be 'extremely infrequently' or 'never'. Arum berries taste disgusting, and they cause such odd tingling sensation on the lips that they're almost impossible to consume in quantity. Humans (and animals) have lived alongside these plants for millennia, so my advice is simply to teach kids to ask before touching, and don't go around snacking on plants you don't recognise. That's what crisps are for.

July brings some of the most intoxicating fragrances of the natural world: **honeysuckle** is in bloom in hedges, **meadowsweet** in damp ditches and fields, and overhead, the **lime trees** (no relation to the citrus fruits) come into bloom. Known as linden trees in Europe, they smell of honey, and in some places, such as Berlin, they spread their fragrance over entire cities. The creamy-white flowers hang down in clusters and are loved by bees and other pollinators, while the leaves are the food plant for several species of moth caterpillars. Lime trees are also a favourite of aphids, which are eaten in turn by ladybirds, hoverflies and birds.

Although much still blooms, spring's vivid green has been replaced by shades of tan, and many of spring's lush weeds are dying back. In cereal-growing parts of the countryside, the **wheat and barley fields turn golden** this month, depending on the weather and when each field was sown; in some parts of the UK the barley and oilseed rape harvest might start, with big combine harvesters out working the fields, though timings are generally later the further north you go.

All the while, both town and countryside are falling quiet. This month the lessening of birdsong becomes marked as many species finish breeding and no longer sing to attract mates or defend territories – though you'll still hear their contact and alarm calls. The dawn chorus is fading away, as is the evening chorus; some birds carry on singing but half-heartedly: the chiffchaff's toy-drum '*dink-dink-dink*' persists, but without the same mad intensity.

Without young to raise – that job being done by poor dunnocks, meadow pipits and the other songbirds whose nests cuckoos lay their eggs in – the adult cuckoos have mostly now left for Africa (brilliantly, you can track the progress of some of Britain's satellite-tagged birds via the British Trust for Ornithology website, an amazing project – see Resources). Their young will follow a few weeks later, setting out to fly 5,000 miles alone, mostly at night, with no experience, no guides and no map.

July 15th is **St Swithin's Day**, when, according to folklore, the next forty days' worth of weather will be predicted: a wet day means forty days of rain – a period that would include the entire harvest – a dry one, forty days of drought. This may seem random, but at one time there were hundreds of superstitions aimed at predicting the weather, which isn't surprising, really, given that people had absolutely no way of knowing what was coming, while at the same time, the literal survival of entire communities was staked on growing food, harvesting it safely and being able to store it for winter. Some forms of weather prognostication were pretty bonkers, but some made sense, such as noting how high swallows flew (insects can be driven lower by approaching storm fronts, meaning swallows swoop lower in pursuit) or whether a pasture looked smooth or rough (clover closes up its leaves before rain, changing the 'nap' of a grassy field). It's a shame that we've largely lost that skill.[4]

If you're watching the weather, keep an eye out after dark for **noctilucent clouds**. This rare phenomenon can occur on any clear summer night in June or July, but is most likely around the first week of July, around an hour or two after sunset. Each cloud is made up of ice particles hanging so high in the atmosphere that they continue to reflect the sun's light long after it's set – hence their name, which means 'night-shining'. They look like otherworldly brushstrokes, glowing at the edge of space.

After St Swithin's Day I start paying special attention to my local blackbird, who only sings now and then, and quietly: one of these recitals will be his last of the year. *How quickly it all passes*, I always find myself lamenting. But how completely precious that makes each moment of the year.

---

4 *The Secret World of Weather* by Tristan Gooley will turn you into a natural weather forecaster.

Each day, note down the very best thing you experienced in the natural world.

Date

Date

Date

Date

Date

Date

Hogweed with red soldier beetle   Ragwort in bloom

BIRD BY EAR

With their strong beaks, yellow wing flashes and olive chests and backs, both male and female greenfinches are handsome birds – though the male's green livery is brighter. They make several sounds, including a rather lovely '*hwit-hwit-hwit-hwit-hwit*', but the one we're concerned with here – because it's the most distinctive – is the wheeze. It's a single, hoarse, descending note, like an outbreath, and to me it always sounds as though they've had a look at you, down below, you foolish human, and are faintly disappointed in you. Hear it enough times in a single day and you may start questioning your life choices.

☐ *Cinnabar moth*   ☐ *Rosebay willowherb*   ☐ *Knapweed*

> *A large, twiggy mass in a tree might be a squirrel's drey, if it's fairly close to the trunk; if it's out among the branches it's more likely to be a magpie's nest.*

Ragwort and hogweed

 ☐ *Buddleia*   ☐ *Took part in the Big Butterfly Count*

Date

Date

Date

Date

Date

Date

☐ *Tried some Solitary Bee Week activities*   ☐ *Dragonfly*   ☐ *Hobby*

Date

Date

Date

Date

Date

Date

🔍 ☐ *Flying ants*　☐ *Grasshopper (seen)*　☐ *Cricket (heard)*

Hobbies are agile enough to catch dragonflies over water

For many plant-lovers, sharing and swapping is a key part of gardening culture. If a neighbour has a plant that you admire, why not ask them if it would grow well from a cutting, or whether they might save you some seeds?

☐ *Orange berries of lords-and-ladies* ☐ *Honeysuckle in bloom*

The common green grasshopper

Give in to the impulse to play: climb trees, build a den, swing on a rope swing, create passing patterns from fallen leaves. Play is a powerful, meaningful and underrated way to connect to the natural world.

 ☐ Meadowsweet ☐ Lime tree fragrance ☐ Jersey tiger moth

Date

Date

Date

Date

Date

Date

☐ *Golden wheat or barley fields* ☐ *Noted the weather on St Swithin's Day*

Date

Date

Date

Moths and butterflies love buddleia –
including hummingbird hawk-moths

BONUS ☐ *Noctilucent clouds* Date: _____ ☐ *Hummingbird hawk-moth*

Date

Date

Date

Date

If you're going pond-dipping, take sunglasses with polarised lenses. They'll help you see past the surface reflections to the underwater world below.

☐ *First ripe tomatoes* Date: _____   ☐ *Pulled up Himalayan balsam*

August

*Harvest time in the fields,
the hedgerows and for garden
veg-growers too – but the
birds have fallen quiet*

When I was a child I thought August was the high point of the year – not because I grew up on a farm and helped gather in the harvest, but because that's when the school holidays were, plus it was usually hot. It's only as I've got older that I've come to understand that the natural world peaks at midsummer, and by August most plants are setting fruit or seed and slowing down. Unless it's been a particularly wet summer, the grass will have lost its springtime energy, and you won't hear much birdsong, if any at all. The breeding season over, most birds will be moulting into a new set of feathers now. This makes them vulnerable, so they stay quiet and out of sight; it's goodbye at last to our local blackbirds' lovely rooftop recitals, and *au revoir* to the dawn and evening choruses for another year. Still, the moult makes it a good month for **collecting feathers**: nearly all of the tiny, lapis-blue jay feathers I own, I've found in August.

However, there are some birds that remain very active this month, albeit not exactly full of tuneful song. Buzzard chicks leave home around now and can often be heard calling repeatedly, usually from a spot high up in a mature tree. **Juvenile buzzards' high, plaintive screams** often come in groups of three and can continue for several hours, which can get quite wearing – not least for the parents, presumably. The chicks want to continue to be fed, but in order to launch them into the world, the parents have to begin withdrawing their care – though they usually won't be far away. Buzzards have suffered several population declines over the years, from persecution by gamekeepers to poisoning with DDT, a now-banned pesticide that moved up the food chain and thinned their eggs along with those of many other birds of prey, badly harming their ability to breed. They were also affected by the deliberate introduction of a disease called myxomatosis to the rabbit population, which dramatically reduced their prey. For a while they clung on only in western areas of the country, but these adaptable generalists have been able to bounce back and now breed in every county of the UK, making them our most common raptor.

It's almost impossible to know when you've seen or heard your last swift: one minute they're there, wheeling high overhead or screaming low above your street, the next they're not. Sometimes, cold, wet conditions will send them away, only for some to return if the temperatures rise. But whatever the weather, they're on notice now to migrate, so get ready to miss them. Fortunately, the swallows and house martins, those other mid-air insect-feeders, will stick around for a while yet.

August 1st used to be known as 'Lammas', from 'loaf mass', a day to give thanks for the first loaf baked using flour from the year's newly harvested wheat. Although in some years, and some parts of the UK, harvest time can begin in July and extend well into autumn (and later, for root crops), August can still be thought of as peak harvesting month, so it's worth keeping an eye out for **combine harvesters**[1] working on the fields. It can be a stressful time for farmers, as even today a lot still depends on fine weather. Heavy rain can flatten crops, known as 'lodging', and affect their quality and ultimate sale price, while damp grain needs drying out, which costs money. Smaller farmers, who may not own their own combines, can be particularly vulnerable to bad weather; if they've booked a contractor who can't work that day as it's too wet, they may miss their slot entirely.

....

1   They're called 'combine harvesters' because they combined what were once separate, highly labour-intensive jobs: reaping (cutting the crop, once done by hand with scythes), threshing (removing the kernels of grain from the ear, done by hand with flails) and winnowing (separating the chaff, i.e. the useless parts of the ear, once done by the wind blowing through the double doors of threshing barns).

When harvest is under way I like to see the **bare stubble** the big machines leave behind, which always feels to me like a real turning point. Once again, the contours of the land are revealed that have been hidden for so many months by the growing and maturing crop. It is a foretaste of autumn, and it always gives me a pleasurable thrill.

Back-garden growers are also harvesting this month: tomatoes (how are yours doing?) should be ripening apace as well as courgettes, green and French beans, mangetout, chard and cucumbers; fruit, too, such as plums and damsons, raspberries, currants, some early varieties of apple and other garden crops. Look out for fruit and veg being given away free outside the houses of people with gluts, and at community veg-growing projects and allotments. I often house-sit for friends this month who have a big vegetable patch and I always struggle to keep on top of everything. You've only got to turn your back on a courgette for five minutes and it's a marrow. And then you're both stuffed.

In parks and hedgerows, **blackberries** will be ripening all month and I urge you to get amongst it with your Tupperware. There are few things nicer than a blackberry and apple crumble, or blackberries on your porridge or stirred into your yoghurt – especially if you freeze some and enjoy them in the depths of winter, a powerful little reminder of summer days. Sure, you can buy blackberries in the shops, but you'll miss out on the sense of connection you can get from spying a good bramble bank, keeping an eye on it for optimum ripeness, then staining your fingertips purple while selecting only the blackest and juiciest fruits – not to mention the hit of vitamin C you get from eating them straight from the bush (vitamin C degrades quickly in harvested fruit). Look out for purple plums, damsons and bullaces, which can be hard to tell apart, as well as little blue-black sloes on blackthorn hedges.

You'll probably see a few wasps buzzing around the hedgerow fruit. We generally know what someone means when they say 'wasp', but in fact the familiar common wasp, plague of picnics, is one of over 9,000 species in the UK, some of which are absolutely tiny, or look nothing like our stripy friends. I always smile to myself when someone asks 'What is the point of wasps?' It shows that they think of everything in the natural world as having a job to do which should be of direct or indirect benefit to humans. That kind of thinking is often described as 'anthropocentric': it puts our species at the centre of everything, which to me is an old-fashioned, knee-jerk belief that's led to a great deal of harm. Wasps are wasps, and they do waspy things, which they have every right to do. They have a vital place in the complex web of life that surrounds us – no more or less than anything else. But if you really *must* think in anthropocentric terms, they're pollinators, for one thing, and they efficiently control the numbers of flies, aphids and other insects in parks and gardens that might otherwise balloon out of control.

In some years, trees may show a small, late flush of new leaves around now, which is known as '**Lammas growth**': look for it on oaks particularly, as their new leaves are often russet-coloured, making it easy to spot. You may see it on ashes, sycamores, beech, hawthorn and other species, too. **Rowan berries** start turning red and orange this month, though they won't be ripe enough for birds to eat just yet; you may even see the rowan's leaves beginning to show their first autumn tints.

Scarlet poppies still dot the fields and roadsides in some parts of the country, though they look less vigorous now than they did earlier in the year. Look out for some of the later-flowering wildflowers, such as **toadflax**, which looks like a small yellow snapdragon, **harebells** – widely known as bluebells in Scotland – **yarrow**, **common agrimony** and **wild carrot**. This last one is another member of the umbellifer[2] (umbrella-like) family, along with cow parsley (in flower April and May) and the hogweed we met last month, but it's shorter, and stands out due to the red central floret within each white flower head and the way its spent flower heads close up into tight little fists like birds' nests. These can persist for months and work well in autumnal flower arrangements, if that's your sort of thing.

One of the real markers of August for me is **thistledown**. The seeds of prickly thistles come with little silky hairs which help to catch the breeze so they can be dispersed as widely as possible, and this month you can often glimpse them drifting through the sunlit air. You can also see thistledown still in situ, handfuls of pewter-coloured down topping the stiff and bristly thistle stems. The seeds are huge favourites of birds like goldfinches and greenfinches, and you might see flocks of them feeding or flying up from stands of thistles as you approach. The reduction in 'weeds' like thistles, dock, nettles and teasels due to modern herbicides is one of the key drivers of farmland bird declines.

Remember the little **holly blue butterfly** we met back in April? Depending on the dramatic yearly fluctuations that this species undergoes,[3] a second generation should be on the wing everywhere but Scotland, from where it's absent. This generation of females will lay their eggs on ivy – specifically on the flower buds. When they hatch, the caterpillars will

....

2 There are actually several more white umbellifers, but let's not make life unnecessarily hard for ourselves.

3 The reason for these fluctuations is thought to be a parasitoid wasp whose sole host is the holly blue caterpillar. Parasite–host relationships are widespread, natural and vital to healthy ecosystems – just as natural as a fungus growing on dead wood or an otter eating a fish.

eat the buds and soft new leaves, eventually overwintering as chrysalises – another reason not to remove ivy over winter. Look out for the adult butterflies in parks and gardens now; they may also lay eggs on spindle, dogwood and bramble.

August is also a good time to spot the beautiful, day-flying **garden tiger moth**. With its leopard-print forewings and spotty orange underwings, it's a real showstopper – as is its huge, hairy caterpillar, usually known as the 'woolly bear'. The caterpillars eat nettles, dock, burdock and other weeds, and while it can still be found across the UK, its numbers are falling – thought to be due to our increasing desire to make everything so neat and tidy, rather than allowing a bit of the bushiness and wildness which nature needs. We could have so many more beautiful creatures like the garden tiger moth if we just relaxed a bit and loosened our death grip on the natural world. And stopped strimming everything.

The **elephant hawk-moth** caterpillar is one of the largest in the UK. Smooth and either lime green or bark-patterned brown, they can be up to 8cm long and boast a sort of horn-like structure in their final segment, making the whole contraption look like a mobile trunk with a trunk. Just behind the head they also have a pair of spots that look like eyes, and they can rear up and swell their top ends to make these eye spots stand out and scare off predators. They eat several plants, including rosebay willowherb, fuchsias and, best of all, the recently arrived Himalayan balsam, giving hope that this problematic plant may one day be brought under natural control.

If you agree with me that moths are hipster butterflies, you might want to try a night-time **moth lure**. This isn't about trapping or harming them but attracting them so you can get a look. Some people simply leave overripe, browning banana skins in their garden and go out after dark to see what's feeding on the inside layer, but there are recipes online for concoctions of banana, brown sugar, cola and treacle which you can paint on to trees or fences. I've seen people have astonishing success with moth lures, but when I tried it, I'm sad to say I got absolutely nothing. Still, there's always next year!

Grasshoppers and crickets are still zithering away: keep listening out, particularly for crickets at dusk. When I lived in south London I remember a summer when one of my neighbours had an invisible Roesel's bush-cricket in their weedy front garden which chirped all night, lending the scruffy, terraced street a pleasingly tropical feel. There should still be loads of butterflies on the wing, and do keep enjoying the gorgeously coloured dragonflies which will continue to zip around like tiny drones all month. A world peopled with all kinds of insects is such a lovely, summery thing, and a stark contrast to how things will feel in December and January, when not much stirs.

Running throughout the summer, the **Bugs Matter** citizen science project is by now in its final month so do join in if you've got a car. Simply download the free app (iOS or Android), then use it to log each car journey; at your destination, use the 'virtual splat-o-meter' to take a photo of your number plate and enter how many dead insects are on it. In 2023, over 6,500 journeys were recorded, providing valuable data. The decline in bug splats on our cars is one of the starkest ways in which recent, dramatic falls in insect numbers have become evident – but it is also a vital way of keeping track of local populations and how they may be affected by the weather and climate change.

Though it's possible to find fungi all year round, autumn is their peak season, when the soil is damp and there's lots of organic matter rotting down. Appearing well ahead of that peak is **fly agaric**, which I usually see for the first time in August. Growing mainly near pines, spruces and birch trees, but also in other woodlands, its fruiting body is our most recognisable mushroom, being bright red and decorated with white spots: a round ball when young, then opening up to a flat cap up to 20cm in diameter. Its colouration is a warning that it's poisonous, so don't go poking at it or letting your dog eat it; however, it's a great subject for photos, particularly if you get right down to ground level. Fly agaric is eaten by red squirrels and reindeer, both of which seem to be immune to its toxins; it's also consumed by fungus gnats and slugs.

Summer is the most likely time for thunderstorms in the UK. Lightning helps plants grow by joining nitrogen to oxygen to form nitrogen dioxide, which dissolves in rain to form nitric acid that is washed into the soil by rain as growth-boosting nitrates. Many people say they can smell storms coming, and it's not such an odd thought: lightning creates ozone, which does have a very particular sharp, seaside smell. And if you get a sudden deluge following a hot, dry spell, go outdoors and breathe in the glorious fragrance known as **petrichor** which is released by rain on dry earth. Like the smell of cut grass (generated by a chemical called coumarin) it triggers strongly positive emotional responses in many people, ranging from a deep sense of nostalgia to utter peacefulness. Some evolutionary psychologists have suggested that these positive associations date from a time when rain and the action of grazing herds will have been crucial to human survival, but I think it's more about simple biophilia. We have loved the living world and its processes for millennia, and that feeling can still be triggered deep in our ancient, lizard brains.

August brings one of the year's real treats: a spectacular meteor shower known as the **Perseids**. Although the Perseids start in July, they peak around the middle of August, and given that warm summer nights are relatively comfortable for skygazing, more people tend to enjoy them than the Geminids, which will arrive in December. Try to choose a night with the least moonlight, so that the meteors will show up better, and if you can, get away from street lights and other urban light pollution. Shooting stars can appear in any part of the sky, and may be as frequent as ninety per hour. The meteors are made up of the debris of a comet known as 109P/Swift-Tuttle, which last appeared in 1992 and will return in 2126, when it'll be visible with the naked eye.

I *love* meteor-watching: it gives me that cosmic shiver that reminds me that I'm a small, short-lived mammal clinging on to an ancient, unique and accidentally beautiful sphere of galactic debris. Oh, and if you do see a falling star this month, don't forget to make a wish.

Each day, note down the very best thing you experienced in the natural world.

Date

Date

Date

Date

Date

Date

🔍 ☐ *Identified feathers*   ☐ *Heard a juvenile buzzard*

BIRD BY EAR

With so few birds in song, and many of the summer visitors preparing to depart, it's time to tune our ears to another kind of avian sound. Both urban and wood pigeons can use their wings on take-off to make a clapping sound; this works as a highly effective alarm, though it's also used during courtship. It's made by the stiff primary feathers striking together when the pigeon's wings are swung up behind their head, and may be accompanied by a whistle, also produced by specialised feathers. Other birds are highly attuned to these wing-claps, and will also take off at the sound.

☐ *Spotted a combine harvester working*   ☐ *Stubble or ploughed fields*

> *Create a map of your garden, park or 'home patch', showing trees, nests, burrows, dens, ponds and other natural features. It doesn't have to be fancy; nobody's marking your work. But it will help you form a meaningful connection to place.*

Blackberries don't all ripen at once

 ☐ *Collected blackberries*   ☐ *Red or orange rowan berries*

Date

Date

Date

Date

Date

Date

☐ *Lammas growth on trees*   ☐ *Toadflax*   ☐ *Yarrow*

Date

Date

Date

Date

Date

Date

  Common agrimony *Harebells* *Wild carrot 'nests'*

Garden tiger moth

If you plan to walk at night, or go stargazing, try setting your phone to 'red mode' so you can use it without harming your night vision. This is part of the accessibility settings; you can find instructions online.

☐ *Thistledown*   ☐ *Holly blue butterfly*   ☐ *Garden tiger moth*

Goldfinches love thistle seeds!

To restore a crumpled feather, hold it in the steam from a kettle's spout for a few seconds. Then pinch and stroke the barbs outwards from the central vane, so they zip back together. Don't burn your fingers!

☐ *Elephant hawk-moth caterpillar*   ☐ *Smelled petrichor*

Date

Date

Date

Date

Date

Date

☐ *Fly agaric mushroom*   ☐ *Watched the Perseid meteor shower*

Date

Date

Date

Fly agaric

Date

Date

Date

Date

Found a pine cone that's been gnawed to its
axis? If there's a tuft left at the top, it was eaten
by a squirrel: those top scales are where it held
the cone. If only a woody stalk is left it was
eaten by a small rodent like a mouse or vole.

September

*As the warmth wanes we say
goodbye to many of our summer
birds. Insects begin their retreat
and the trees take on colour*

I once heard someone say that the only people who love autumn are the ones who were swots as kids, and that everyone else dreads it as a reminder of the new school year. Well, I was both a swot *and* someone who dreaded going back to school, and I love September almost as much as I love May. And that goes to show that there are never only two types of person in the world, unless it's the type of person who wants to reduce life's rich tapestry to binaries, and the rest of us who know how feeble-minded that is.

I love September for the feeling of change in the air. By the middle of August, I'm often sick of the heat, and if it hasn't been warm, I'll be tired of the feeling of stasis that can creep over the natural world. The grass isn't growing; the trees' leaves look dull and tired; the birds have been in moult and are rarely seen. One day can feel much like the next, and I usually find myself itching for the spell to break and things to start moving forwards again – even for chilly mornings and frosts and winter jumpers, though I know that come February I'll have had enough of those things again.

In September I love picking up brand-new **conkers** and taking them home, so glossy and irresistible in their waxy vernix, yet so quick to turn dull. I love watching the **leaves change colour**, and, in a good year, remain on the trees, blazing out across the landscape in reds, oranges and golds. Cooler nights and falling light levels cause chlorophyll – the green pigment – in leaves to break down, revealing the colours of the other, underlying pigments: the xanthophylls and carotenoids, and, in species such as maples (and more widely if the weather conditions have been just right), the bright red anthocyanins, a marker of high sugar levels in the tree's sap. Unlike spring, which arrives first to the south of the UK, autumn arrives first in the north and moves down. Often the first indications of what kind of year it'll be for foliage can be seen in Scotland, so it's worth keeping an eye on conditions there.

I've known years that have been a bit 'meh' when it comes to autumn colour, years when the leaves haven't turned until November, and others when the trees have been utterly spectacular all through September: day after day of heart-lifting colour from every forest, wood and humble street tree, with no wind to tear them down. If you're lucky enough to get a year like that, make sure you get out and enjoy it as much as possible: the autumn that follows might not be anything like as good.

The **autumn equinox** falls around the 22nd of this month: the moment when the hours of darkness will exceed those of light. I usually mark it by lighting a candle, and will light one every evening until Christmas: not a fancy scented one, just the kind you can buy in packs of six from the supermarket, for a couple of quid.

By the equinox the autumn migration, which began in August with swifts, seabirds and waders, will be reaching its peak. It's the second of the year's great avian population shifts, though it can feel less dramatic: without the urge to arrive quickly and set up a breeding territory, birds slip away gradually, often overnight, and sometimes make several stops along the way. Willow warblers, whitethroats, reed warblers, garden warblers – all the UK's warblers will leave, flying mostly in the dark, bar two: the little Dartford warbler, rare and very vulnerable to a hard winter here at the northerly edge of its European range; and Cetti's warbler, a real loudmouth of a bird that's only recently colonised parts of England, and which eats aquatic invertebrates and their larvae. In recent years, and mostly in the Southeast, blackcaps are beginning to chance their arm and stay, though the UK's population is still considered migratory; they'll switch their diet from bugs, which (as I'm sure you've noticed) are on the wane in September, to berries, particularly mistletoe. In these last examples you can see the way that climate change is already altering the biodiversity of the UK.

Swallows gather on wires, preparing themselves; like swifts and house martins, they'll migrate in the daytime, hoovering up insects as they go. In place of the departing warblers and other songbirds will come the thrushes: redwings and fieldfares here for the winter. **Redwings** mass along the Scandinavian coast at dusk before launching off on their single 500-mile flight across the North Sea to the UK; they can be heard after dark on cold autumn nights, calling to one another in the blackness overhead with their high '*tseep! tseep!*' calls, something I've always listened out for and found magical – even in the heart of London. The fact that so many birds travel at night is extraordinary to me, especially when they do so over huge bodies of water. Picture it: dark, choppy water stretching out to every horizon, the black, starlit sky overhead. And in it, millions of little, feathered bodies streaming landwards, their little hearts beating, their eyes open wide.

In fact, there's nothing about these huge avian journeys that isn't utterly extraordinary, and I urge you to read up[1] about migration. The British Trust for Ornithology (BTO) website has a dedicated section with some fascinating articles, plus a blog which goes live during the spring and autumn migrations and keeps people up to date with arriving and departing species, including peak migration nights and good places to see birds on the move.

....

1 *Flight Paths* by Rebecca Heisman is an accessible and awe-inspiring account of what birds do, and how they do it. If you fancy a really deep dive, *Bird Migration* by Ian Newton (Collins New Naturalist series) is the one. The BTO's migration blog is at www.bto.org/our-science/topics/migration

Conkers aren't the only things ripening now: in the hedgerows you'll find **hips** and **haws** (the fruits of dog roses and hawthorns, respectively) and the sour, blue-black fruits of the blackthorn, **sloes**, which may be purple from July but are only ripe when soft to a squeeze. These can be picked to **make sloe gin**, and if you start now you'll have a batch ready to give as Christmas presents. It's super-easy, and you can find recipes online: all you need – apart from sloes – is gin and sugar. There's something really special about drinking an SG&T made from hedgerow fruits you picked yourself, and which began as some of the earliest blossoms you saw way back in March.

Even earlier than that, in February, we looked for lambs' tails, the yellowy-green catkins of hazel. Now's the time to return to that tree, as its **hazelnuts** should be ripe and delicious – those that haven't been eaten by squirrels, that is, which are happy to tuck in while they're still green. On **rowan** trees both in the countryside and so commonly planted in cities, bright orangey-scarlet berries have appeared, and these will be important food for birds as the weather turns colder. Female yew trees also produce fruit at this time of year: technically called **arils**, rather than berries, they look like little red fairy lights amid the dark needles of this tough, evergreen and exceptionally long-lived tree. Often found in churchyards, some yews might actually be older than the church building itself: one in Scotland, known as the Fortingall Yew, is thought to be 5,000 years old.

Hopefully last month you found your first fly agaric of the year, and perhaps, if the ground was damp, more **mushrooms** too. Come September, depending on local conditions, you should see more and more appearing on your walks – either on the ground, on the trunks of trees or on rotting wood.

In many countries, children are taught which species are good to eat, and as adults will harvest them each autumn as naturally as we go blackberrying; in the UK we've largely lost our confidence with fungi, something I think is a great shame. If you'd like to forage, have a look online and in the local press to see if there are any guided walks planned in your area. Learning in real life, and from an expert, is by far the best way, as fungi can be variable and don't always look like photos on apps, online or even in books. Some species are highly poisonous and, unlike other potentially harmful plants that rarely, if ever, actually do anyone any harm, illness and even death *do* occur in relation to fungi, usually because people mistake an edible species for a close mimic.

Nevertheless, these weird life forms are completely fascinating – even if, like me, you don't intend to forage. There are 15,000 species in the UK alone, which is staggering, and we're only just scratching the surface in terms of understanding what they are and what they do.[2] A few I like to look out for in autumn are the stinkhorn, or witch's egg, which appears in woods, extends upwards from a white sphere in the leaf litter to a slimy-capped phallus, and which absolutely *reeks*; the giant puffball, which swells in grassy fields, releases up to seven trillion spores, and could easily be mistaken for an abandoned football; beefsteak fungus, which looks like (you guessed it) a raw steak someone's stapled to the trunk of an oak or sweet chestnut tree; and the orange peel fungus, which again is very descriptively

---

2 I highly recommend *Entangled Life: How Fungi Make Our Worlds, Change our Minds and Shape Our Futures* by Merlin Sheldrake. It's brilliant – one of those books that make your head wobble (in a good way).

named and usually appears on bare soil such as ploughland or the edges of paths, though sometimes in grass. Look out for **fairy rings**, too, particularly after wet weather: circles of mushrooms which spread outwards each year, so the bigger the ring, the older the underground network. Even when no fruiting bodies are visible above ground, you might see a ring of greener grass as the mycelia release nitrogen and other nutrients into the earth. Around 60 per cent of the world's species live in soil, including 90 per cent of all fungi; healthy soil is fundamental to everything from carbon storage and climate regulation to global food production. We need to think a lot harder about how we can protect and preserve it, rather than treating it as an inert 'growing medium'.

In many parts of the country, and depending on the weather, the cereal harvest will continue into September. In fact, in the olden days this was the peak month for harvesting; modern crop varieties, fertilisers, chemicals and agricultural techniques allowing earlier sowing and faster ripening have brought it forward. It's why the full moon around the end of September and start of October is called the **Harvest Moon**: often the extra light across several nights as the moon waxed full and then waned would allow labourers to work on after dark, getting everything safely gathered in. It's a great opportunity for another night walk: first have a look at the magical moonlit paintings of Samuel Palmer, then go out and enjoy the feeling of an autumnal night.

In churches across the country a Harvest Festival service may still be held, with donations of food to go to local food banks or other charities. These services are the last remnant of a huge annual celebration, different in each county, that would have involved everyone who lived in the countryside – which, of course, used to be most of the population. Harvest feasts and rituals were a way of celebrating a good harvest, bringing a community together, strengthening bonds and thanking workers for their labour; some ceremonies, such as casting a sickle at the last standing sheaf or making a corn dolly from the final stems of wheat, may have their roots in pre-Christian times.

In the animal world, too, much harvesting is taking place as the last of the wild food must be eaten or stored before winter: wood mice will be caching seeds, berries and nuts in burrows, hollow stumps and crevices in the bases of hedges, while moles will bite the heads off worms and store them alive in underground larders. Meanwhile, hedgehogs need to get up to about 600g in order to survive hibernation, so between now and November they need to roam widely, without being squished on roads, and find as many invertebrates to eat as possible. If you have hogs in your area, and you don't have a rat problem, you could lend a helping hand by **putting out hedgehog food** (or kitten food in a chicken flavour – but not the kind in gravy). Offer a bowl of fresh water too, ideally in a box that prevents cats or other creatures getting in and nicking it. You can find examples online.

I always used to notice a downturn in my dog Scout's behaviour in September: her recall, in particular, seemed to take six steps back. Eventually we connected it to the fact that almost everywhere we walked her, **grey squirrels** were more visible and distracting: instead of staying in the branches, they were down on the ground burying acorns, nuts and things they'd found in bins – the source of the phrase 'squirrelling away'. Jays are also great acorn-buriers, and we'll learn more about them next month.

Grey squirrels were deliberately introduced to the UK from America in 1876, and with them a virus to which they were immune but our native red squirrel was not – resulting in the unintended loss of reds, now hanging on only in parts of northern England, in Scotland and Ireland, and on Brownsea Island and the Isle of Wight.

Greys damage trees by chewing the bark off all the way around the trunk, resulting in the death of the tree; some ecologists believe that it will be very difficult to achieve our tree planting (and carbon capture) goals with the numbers of grey squirrels we currently have. In many areas, measures are in place to reduce grey squirrel numbers, while research is ongoing into whether it might be possible to reduce breeding by targeted feeding with contraceptives.

Three of the UK's deer species start their mating season in late September (roe deer rut in close, muggy weather in July and August). **The rut** is when male red, fallow and sika deer compete to win a harem of females to mate with, and it can be quite dramatic. A staple of wildlife TV, you might be familiar with footage of red deer stags clashing antlers, proudly carrying around clumps of bracken and weeds on their heads and wallowing in mud and urine (the hormones in their wee bring the females into heat – hey, each to their own, I'm not judging). If you'd like to witness a deer rut, have a look at your local Wildlife Trust site and join a guided walk. There are also deer parks across the country with captive populations, but make sure you keep dogs on a short lead and don't get too close: pumped up males can be dangerous. Most activity is around dawn and dusk, but you may see stags or bucks pacing up and down and facing off at any time. And if you live in a rural area, keep your ears peeled at dusk and overnight for the unearthly sound of roaring and bellowing. The shiver it'll give you is like the last, atavistic memory of the time we spent living with megafauna like aurochs, elk, mammoths and cave lions.

In the countryside, the partridge shooting season starts on September 1st, while for pheasants, it's October 1st. Although

small numbers of pheasants have become naturalised in the UK, the vast majority are bred in captivity and released annually to be shot. Releases take place in early autumn, and if you live in, or regularly drive through, areas where shoots are held you might notice **young pheasants** running about all over the place, most of whom have very little road sense. One study found that 40 per cent of carcasses reported on the UK's roads were of pheasants. I've hit one myself, and I can tell you: it wasn't a pleasant experience.

In town and countryside alike, some – but not all – **juvenile foxes** begin to leave their home territories around now, and will continue to disperse during the next couple of months. More males leave their parents' patches than females, presumably in search of a mate; however, striking out instead of staying put is a risky strategy, resulting in shorter life expectancy. There is often a spike in road deaths of young foxes around this time.

As the night skies start to get longer and darker following the autumn equinox, it's a good time for stargazing, and in September the constellation of **Cygnus**, or the Swan, appears roughly overhead. Once you've located its huge cross pattern – that of a swan diving with neck outstretched – you'll always find it easy to spot. To get started, you could try an app such as Star Walk (see Resources), which uses your location and the position of your phone to become a 'window' on to the skies, showing you the eighty-eight constellations and letting you click on stars, planets and other sky objects to learn more about them. And if you find yourself somewhere with truly dark skies, make sure you look out for the **Milky Way** overhead. Knowing you're gazing out through one of the arms of our galaxy is an experience so mind-blowing, so ancient, yet also so grounding, that it should be on the school curriculum, or on prescription, or somehow officially arranged for every single one of us.

Each day, note down the very best thing you experienced in the natural world.

Date

Date

Date

Date

Date

Date

🔍 ☐ *First ripe conkers on the ground* Date: _____

BIRD BY EAR

The writer Paul Evans has described the sound of a goldfinch flock as that of distant playgrounds. Often seen (and heard) in groups, they have a fast, liquid and frankly delightful song, which often contains the repeated phrase '*tswhitt-whitt-whitt*' and sometimes even a trill – though nothing like the rapid machine-gun trill of a wren. These pretty little finches love tiny seeds such as those of knapweed, cornflower and teasels, but since the widespread use of farmland weedkillers wiped out many of their natural food sources, they've dared more and more to come to gardens – particularly those offering sunflower hearts and nyjer seeds.

☐ *Heard redwings overhead* Date: _____   ☐ *Leaves changing colour*

Animal droppings are one of the best clues when it comes to working out who lives near you. The Wildlife Trusts have a great guide at www.wildlifetrusts.org/wildlife/how-identify/identify-poo

Grey squirrel

 ☐ *Swallows on overhead wires* ☐ *Hips and haws*

Date

Date

Date

Date

Date

Date

☐ *Ripe sloes* ☐ *Rowan berries* ☐ *Collected ripe hazelnuts*

Date

Date

Date

Date

Date

Date

🔍 ☐ *Yew arils* ☐ *Fairy ring* ☐ *Identified a mushroom*

Stinkhorns were once carefully cleared away before
any ladies saw them and found them improper

*Climbing a tree – particularly at dusk – can
be a great way to see wildlife as your scent is
carried above ground level. Be prepared to
sit still, settle in and be patient, though!*

☐ *Harvest Moon*　　☐ *Grey squirrels caching food*　　☐ *Young pheasants*

Pheasants

If you have a garden, try not to tidy it up too much when autumn comes. Dead leaves and old, dry seed-heads provide vital shelter for overwintering insects like ladybirds, as well as harbouring invertebrate eggs and larvae until the weather warms up in spring.

 ☐ *Heard or saw a deer rut*   ☐ *Juvenile fox*   ☐ *The Milky Way*

Date

Date

Date

Date

Date

Date

☐ *Cygnus constellation* ☐ *Marked the autumn equinox*

Date

Date

Date

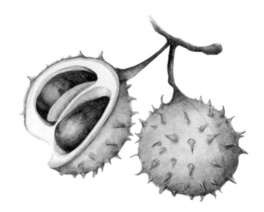

Conkers: glossy and irresistible

🔍 *BONUS* ☐ *Made sloe gin* ☐ *Fed hedgehogs*

Date

Date

Date

*If you're entering a bird hide, tread quietly and
speak softly so as not to scare off any rarities
the people in the hide might be observing.
Do the same when leaving – don't start chatting
loudly the moment you're out of the door!*

October

The natural world begins its
preparations for winter. Birds
arrive, escaping colder places;
the trees reveal themselves

To me, October is to autumn what April is to spring: the month that ushers in the new season, one of the two great hinges of the year. In some years our deciduous trees' leaves fall in September: drought can cause early leaf loss but so can an unseasonal cold snap. Sometimes – and in some parts of the country – they hang on into November, but as a rough guide, October is usually when the bulk of the leaves fall. This helps to protect trees from winter gales, as a canopy in full leaf acts like a sail, trapping the air's energy. People often think that large burdens of ivy kill trees, but that's not the case: what does happen, though, is that an already rotten or weakened tree, full of evergreen ivy, is felled by winter wind.

One of my favourite things to look out for in October is the **prints left by fallen leaves** on pavements. This occurs when wet leaves with high tannin content remain in the same spot long enough for the tannins to leach out into the concrete or artificial stone of the paving slabs. They usually wash away within a week or two, but for the short period they're there, they're well worth taking the time to notice and photograph: ghosts of summer leaves that will never exist again, records of the fleeting form taken by those tight, unfurling buds of spring.

Where drifts of oak leaves lie, look out for the flat little buttons on their undersides, only a few millimetres across, called **spangle galls**. Galls are specialised microhabitats created by plants under the direction of parasites such as flies, beetles or even fungi, and come in many shapes from large, hard spheres to knobbly growths to furry pincushions and weird elves' hats. Spangle galls are formed in autumn to protect the larvae of a tiny wasp less than 4mm long, allowing them to feed on the tissue of the oak leaves;

when the leaves fall, the larvae continue to develop within their galls, eventually hatching out in April. The new, female wasps will then lay eggs in oak catkins, leading to a second, completely distinct generation, which will lay eggs on the leaf undersides again. Although spangle galls can sometimes almost cover the underside of oak leaves, they do almost no damage to the living tree.

The other thing falling from oaks about now is acorns, and many of them will be busily snapped up by hungry **jays**. A member of the corvid family, along with crows and magpies, jays are extremely clever, and they're also absolutely *incredible* at forest regeneration – far better, by some measures, than we are ourselves. In the case of two new woodlands in Cambridgeshire, it was estimated that more than half the trees there were planted by jays.

In autumn, jays will converge on stands of oaks with ripe acorns from all directions – sometimes flying in from several miles away. Some acorns will be eaten, some buried close to the tree, and some carried back to each bird's home range in its crop (a pouch in their gullet) – up to nine acorns at a time. These will be cached in many different locations to provide food through the lean winter months, the spot often marked by a thorny shrub, sapling or tall weed – tall enough to still be visible if it snows – to help their owner remember where they are. Although jays' memories are extremely acute, inevitably, some acorns aren't eaten, and these will often germinate – particularly those 'planted' in scrub or grassland, where they'll get lots of light, rather than in woodland, where acorns would naturally drop. In addition, markers chosen by jays as aide-memoires, such as prickly young hawthorn or holly bushes, often protect tender oak seedlings from being eaten by deer. In this way, jays help oaks spread out from under their own large, dense canopies – and if you find an oak sapling growing out in the open like that, chances are it was planted by a jay.

And here's a cool thing. Jays will move a stash if they think another jay – or a grey squirrel – has seen them bury it; they've also been observed *pretending* to bury acorns, but in fact taking them elsewhere. This is believed by some researchers to show that they have a theory of mind: the ability to attribute mental states to others, for example by perceiving that another being is forming an intention, without seeing them act on it. Other corvids, some apes and dogs are also thought to possess theory of mind, but it's my belief that – as usual – we are wildly underestimating our fellow creatures and that it is in fact very widespread. I wasn't surprised at all when I read about a study showing that squirrels, when caching food, sometimes appear to do the same.

The autumn migration continues into October, so keep your eyes peeled for the **last of the year's swallows**, mixed flocks of departing warblers and other small birds, and continue to listen out at night for redwings flying overhead. Numbers of many familiar garden birds such as blackbirds and starlings will be swelled by more arriving from colder climes, so you might also see an uptick of those in your garden or local park.

Now and again, if we're lucky, we get what's known as a '**waxwing winter**'. This occurs every few years or so, when the population of this garrulous and photogenic bird outstrips the amount of food available in its home range of northern Europe, and an 'irruption' of birds arrives in the UK, particularly along the eastern coastlines and inland from there. They eat berries – those of rowans and hawthorns in particular – and are quite happy to congregate in city streets and supermarket car parks, efficiently stripping the fruit from shrubs and trees and posing for photos. If you hear of some arriving near you, it's well worth going out to see if you can find them; they can be quite fearless and will often let you get pretty close. With their shark-fin crests and neat, fluoro trims, they look like the souped-up rally version of some much less interesting LBJ (little brown job).

Though sometimes starting in late September, October usually sees the biggest influx of wintering waterfowl: keep your eyes on the skies and you might see **geese flying in long, straggling Vs and lines**. For big birds, flying in a formation like that helps them make better progress: they can get up to 70 per cent further than a single bird flying alone. If they time their wing flaps right, each bird except the leader gets a boost of upwashed air from the one flying in front; after a while, the hardworking lead bird will drop back and let someone else take a turn.

We host several species of geese over winter, including barnacle, brent, greylag, pink-footed, Russian and Greenland white-fronted, and the Taiga bean and Tundra bean geese. Brent geese arrive in early October, one race – the dark-bellied – in southern and eastern England, and the other – the pale-bellied – mostly in Ireland. The UK's Canada geese – familiar and widespread, with the black head and neck – are largely sedentary, though some do move around in order to complete their summer moult somewhere safe.

Pink-footed geese are particularly loud while in the air, like the belling of distant hounds, and the sound is a real marker of winter. If you'd like to experience it, the Montrose Basin in Angus often plays host to tens of thousands in October and November, with huge flocks at Cley Marshes in Norfolk, Spurn and Staveley in Yorkshire, and other wetland sites too. Once they have arrived here from Iceland and eastern Greenland they move around a lot, looking for good places to roost and graze, so you may well catch sight of a flock on the move.

Wigeon are another winter visitor: a small but exceedingly handsome duck. Although very few breed in northern Scotland, most begin to arrive here in September with the main influx in October and into November, and our total winter population is an estimated 450,000 birds. They like to hang out together and can often be seen in large flocks in coastal areas like estuaries and mudflats, floating on lakes and reservoirs, or grazing grass inland. One of the things I love about wigeon is the fact that they can't quack: instead, the males rather sweetly go '*Pew! Peewwww! Peeew! Pew!*' repeatedly, which, when multiplied by several hundred in a flock, is an extraordinary sound. They'll leave again come March, so take the chance to seek them out before then, if you'd like to.

The flat, papery **seed pods of honesty** have been ripening and then desiccating since midsummer, and now, as the two outer layers fall to release the seeds, the silvery, translucent inner membrane is revealed: nacreous, like mother-of-pearl. I like to grow honesty in my garden for its early spring flowers and as food for pollinators, but it's the seed discs I love best, glimmering in the shadows under hedges or beside roads, or adding interest to an otherwise emptying flower bed. This wildflower's common names refer either to the moon, as in moonwort (its Latin name is *Lunaria*) or the seeds' similarity to money: money plant, Peter's pence, penny flower, two-pennies-in-a-purse and money-in-both-pockets are just some. I tend to keep my eye on any good clumps in sheltered places, and in October, once the seeds that'll make a new generation have fallen, I'll bring the brittle, beautiful stems with their dangling discs inside to enjoy over winter, perhaps with some empty **teasels**, dried **quaking grass** or other souvenirs of the season past.

Another reminder of the summer comes in the form of **ripe apples**, with **Apple Day** celebrated on October 21ˢᵗ. Thanks to supermarkets and international shipping, we have largely lost the sense of apples as a seasonal fruit, like strawberries, but for generation upon generation they ripened largely in autumn, and could either be enjoyed fresh straight away, preserved, or carefully stored for eating over winter; varieties of apple were bred to ripen at staggered times from late July to spring, or to store well. One cultivar, little grown now, was rumoured to keep for two years.

Apples are extremely heterozygous, meaning that every pip will grow into a different tree with unique characteristics (and fruit). This makes them utterly fascinating to grow, and they were bred – mostly by the Victorians, who adored them – to suit local conditions right across the country, leading to wide variations in colour, size, taste, use, shelf life, fragrance and even vitamin C levels. Around 2,500 varieties have been cultivated in this country, and that's not even counting cider apples.

Although they arrived here with the Romans from the China–Kazakhstan border area, apples have a strong case to be our national fruit. It's a huge shame that so many are now lost as we no longer value them, something that Apple Day aims to combat. Some cultivars, however, are unlikely to disappear: every single Bramley apple, the UK's most popular cooking apple, comes from a tree that will have originated from grafts of a single tree in Southwell, Nottinghamshire – now 200 years old (an incredible age for an apple tree), blown over by a storm and struck by lightning, but still producing fruit.

'Wildings' flourish too, each one unique, from the cores we drop or throw out of car windows – though I was surprised to learn that throwing fruit out of a car window is not without its environmental impact. The 'apple core effect' describes the needless deaths of owls and other raptors attracted to roadsides by the rodents feeding there, and then being hit by traffic – those rodents attracted to the verge in turn by the food we throw out of cars. Obviously, throwing litter out of car windows would be punishable by instant death in my glorious kingdom, but I'd always thought the odd apple core was no bad thing. I'll be taking them back to my wormery in future.

This is peak **flowering time for ivy**. This common evergreen climber puts out creamy-green blooms in little starburst-type globes, like rather chic pendant lights for a 1960s doll's house, and their fragrance is... well, it really is something. Some people don't mind it, some absolutely hate it, but once I tell you that it's often compared to semen, I promise you won't forget it.[1] Bees love the flowers, though, which is what's important: ivy is a crucial source of late food for many insects before they go into hibernation, when not much else around is flowering. In fact, in recent years it's even got its own specialist assistant, the **ivy bee**. First recorded in the UK in 2001, ivy bees are now widespread in southern England and are moving north. They nest underground, usually in light, sandy soil, and emerge around September time, ready for ivy to begin flowering. Oh, and do keep an eye on that ivy you've been sniffing: the berries come next, which are also key.

Sightings of house spiders increase in autumn. Rather than this being because they all rush indoors to keep out of the cold, it's mainly due to the fact that as their breeding season commences, males begin to move around, looking for a mate

---

1 I mentioned ivy's characteristic fragrance in a piece I wrote for a national newspaper, but – disappointingly, I thought – it was edited out.

– and so we see them more. My mum would scream at the sight of spiders, and my dad would pick them up and sometimes chase us kids around with them; I've worked hard to outgrow the reactions I learnt as a child, because they're not rational or useful to me. However, for true arachnophobes – rather than the majority of us who just don't appreciate the scuttling – I know that's not possible. Still, they do help keep down flies, mosquitoes, clothes moths and other unwelcome beasties, and if you take the time to learn a bit more about them, you may find your interest and curiosity helps overcome any aversion you have.

A good place to start is with the **garden spider**, which matures in late summer and autumn. A type of orb-weaver – the group that spins the beautiful symmetrical webs we always think of in connection with arachnids – they're both common and easily recognised, with a fat, rounded body and white cross on their back. They eat their web once a day and then spin a new one, so it's always in good nick and ready to trap flying insects. And at this time of year, moisture often condenses on them overnight, making them sparkle – a great subject for a spot of autumnal photography.

We take spider webs for granted, but they are incredibly complex miracles of engineering and well worth reading up on; researchers are still trying to unlock many of the secrets of their construction. But not all the research has been that revelatory: in the 1970s an American scientist dosed some unfortunate spiders with a range of drugs, from caffeine to LSD. The results were predictable: on speed the webs were 'highly irregular and unstructured', while on LSD the spiders' capabilities were either 'completely disrupted' or altered to the point where the webs actually became three-dimensional.

I have to say, I feel sorry for the spiders. It's not cool to spike your friends.

Finally, this month, a reminder: it's time to plant your **tulip bulbs**. I like to do mine in pots and tubs[2] – ones with holes in the bottom – for intense bursts of springtime colour. You can pack them in quite closely, around 5cm apart and about 20cm deep, and they'll sort themselves out as they grow. Make sure to choose peat-free compost, and if you have squirrels, foxes, rats or cats you might want to put some chicken wire over the top of the pot to prevent them being plundered, crapped on, or dug up in order to hide things in there. Then water them in, pop the pot somewhere it'll get rained on and forget about it until next year.

---

2 If you'd prefer to plant them in the ground, wait a little longer – ideally until there have been a couple of good frosts. That should kill off any spores of tulip fire, a fungal disease lurking in the soil.

Each day, note down the very best thing you experienced in the natural world.

Date

Date

Date

Date

Date

Date

The last swallow Date: _____

BIRD BY EAR

Man alive, jays make a racket. They have several sounds in their repertoire, but the one I want you to listen out for this month is the call – a hoarse, cracked, ugly sort of shriek: '*Skaaaark... shaaaaaaak!*' Sometimes it's a contact call, and sometimes a warning of danger – usually meaning you – and it's often uttered in flight. It's loud and pretty unmistakable; the caw of a crow is much more pleasant, and magpies are less screechy and more '*ack-ack-ack-ack*'. If I hear the loud screech of a corvid in woodland, I gauge it on my unpleasantness meter, and if it rates high, it'll be a jay.

☐ *Spangle galls on oak leaves*   ☐ *Jays*

If you have a woodburner or open fire, connect with your local area (and your ancestors) by gathering twigs on your walks rather than buying expensive, plastic-packaged kindling. Set them in a basket near your hearth to dry out for a night or two, or hang a string bag in your chimney. Don't take them all, though!

In October, apples are in season

 ☐ *Leaf prints on pavements*   ☐ *Skein of geese*

Date

Date

Date

Date

Date

Date

Honesty seed pods

Date

Date

Date

Date

Date

Date

 ☐ *Teasels* ☐ *Quaking grass bells*

Orb weavers: artisans of autumn

Look for small collections of white and grey droppings: clues to the spots where small birds roost at night. If you can find some roosts in your garden you can protect your birds by allowing foliage to grow there all year round.

☐ *Picked ripe apples*

Winter-visiting wigeon

Discovering a place's history can deepen your relationship with it. Perhaps where you walk was once a grand deer park, or an industrial site; maybe there are remnants of ancient wildwood, agricultural hedges and ditches or mining, all of which will affect the wildlife you see there now.

☐ *Ivy in flower*   ☐ *Web of garden spider*

Date

Date

Date

Date

Date

Date

Date

Date

Date

Jay caching acorns

🔍 *BONUS* ☐ *Wigeons whistling* ☐ *Took part in Apple Day activities*

Date

Date

Date

Date

A patch of ground covered in feathers may be a clue
to a kill. On open ground it could be a kill site, where
a bird was pounced on by a predator or hit from
above by a bird of prey. In woodland, they might have
drifted down from a plucking post high in a tree.

☐ Waxwings   ☐ Ivy bees   ☐ Planted tulip bulbs

November

As the light fails and fades,
the story of November is one of
disappearance and decay. The
first frosts spell death for the
adult forms of many insects

November opens with the ancient festival of Samhain, when some believe the veil between this world and the next is at its thinnest. The days are darkening and the earth cooling; ice can grip it easily now, and it will. Gardeners up and down the country worry about **the first frost** as it can kill tender plants that didn't evolve for our conditions; these must be brought inside or into greenhouses or cold frames, wrapped in fleece, or mulched to insulate their roots. Pots can make some plants more vulnerable as the cold comes in from all directions, so do keep an eye on the forecast or set an overnight temperature alert on the weather app on your phone. And remember: cold weather can be necessary for good garden health, killing off pests and pathogens which can survive a mild winter, ready to surge up, redoubled, in spring. It also puts paid to most biting flies. Frost also softens and sweetens some fruits so they're ready to eat, by a process called 'bletting': quinces and medlars, for example, which are hard, tart and inedible before the first frost but delicious afterwards.

I'm slightly obsessed with taking **photos of frost** before it melts: there's something about the way it carefully outlines in silver even the humblest weed stalk or dead leaf that stops me in my tracks and makes everything I look at feel extraordinary and precious – which, of course, it is.

At last, the big deciduous trees are bare and we can see the shape their branches make against iron-grey skies. Look out for the ash, whose beckoning terminal twigs we admired back in February; in cities, see the way **plane trees**, with their flaky, camo-patterned bark, are hung with round seed pods like Christmas baubles; find an old and broad-trunked **oak** and admire its spreading crown and the way the branches, strong enough sometimes to be held out horizontally, twist and bend as though to seek the light.

November is a good time to look out for **dogwood**, too, a shrub that grows wild in hedgerows in the south of England but is also loved by gardeners and florists for its brightly coloured, straight young twigs in shades of red, orange and yellow. When its leaves fall, these blaze out and can look astonishing from a distance, as though the whole hedge is on fire.

Earlier in autumn we saw the fruiting bodies of secretive fungal networks appear in public as mushrooms and release their spores, but underground, mycelial networks are at work all year, helping trees and plants share nutrients and information, protecting them from disease, locking away 75 per cent of the world's terrestrial carbon and recycling vital substances that power life on earth. At this time of year, many fungi are busy breaking down the waste products of the growing season – spent leaves, seed pods, fruit, twigs, old bits of bark, dead wood and dead invertebrates, as well as moulted feathers, dead birds and other creatures – so that their nutrients can be made available to power the next year's cycle of growth. This is the shadow side of spring's mad uprush and it is every bit as important. We imagine decay to be about endings when really it is all about new life.

Fungi are aided in this work by **detritivores**: invertebrates like woodlice, worms, millipedes and beetles that break up organic matter ready for fungi and bacteria to process. If you turn over some nice damp leaf litter, you'll see it's full of these kinds of creatures, all hard at work. That's why, if you have a garden or help out in a park, one of the best things you can do is leave plant matter to decay naturally, instead of bagging it all up, resorting to ecocidal leaf blowers[1] or carbon dioxide- and particulate-releasing bonfires. Natural detritus like seed heads, hollow stems and shed bark also provide safe shelter for eggs, larvae and chrysalises of next year's moths and butterflies, so when you remove it all, not only are you depriving your soil of potential nutrients, you're banishing vast numbers of vital living things. Whether you have a window box or a country estate, take pride in how busy and rich its operations of decay are, as well as the more obvious processes of growth that take place earlier in the year. One fuels the other, after all.

A good compromise is to gently rake up only the leaves that you really must – from your lawn, say, but not your flower beds – and either scatter them somewhere else or make leaf mulch from them which you can then spread back on to the soil next year. You don't need a mulching machine, a shop-bought bin or fancy structure to make it, either: I use a few old plastic sacks saved from when I've bought peat-free compost earlier in the year. I stab holes in the bottoms so they don't fill with water, pop in fallen leaves (no trees overhang my garden, so I nick them from the edges of our village lanes), leave the tops open to the elements and stick them round the back of the shed. By the following autumn, I'll have free bags of crumbly, organic soil improver. Win-win.

Much of the organic detritus rotting down right now derives from herbaceous (leafy) plants whose strategy for surviving winter's rigours is either to set seed and die off (annual and second-year biennial plants) or abandon all their vulnerable above-ground growth and retreat to the underworld, where they will survive as tubers, corms, bulbs

---

1   In Germany, the government has told citizens that leaf blowers are contributing to 'insect Armageddon' and should be avoided. According to the charity Buglife, 40 per cent of known insect species face extinction, while nearly 9 per cent of all insects are lost each decade.

or root systems, ready to put out fresh new growth in spring (this is the case for perennials). It's odd to think that when you see a barren-looking flower bed in November, all bare earth and sad fragments of shrivelled gubbins, it might be no less full of plants as it was when it looked riotous and colourful back in June.

And sometimes the detritus is beautiful: the teasels and honesty seed heads we admired last month, for example, but also the ghost-grey, fluffy **seed heads of wild clematis** scrambling through a hedgerow. A favourite of the poet Edward Thomas, who tried to capture it in his poems several times, it's classed as invasive in New Zealand, where it was introduced some time in the last century; here, however, it's the caterpillar food plant for several kinds of moth, and these tend to keep it under control. I suppose it's to New Zealand what Himalayan balsam is to here: a reminder that it's not about a species being inherently bad, it's about whether it can fit into an ecological niche in a new location, prove useful, and be kept under control by other things.

Remarkably, there are a few native plants that seem at their most vigorous at this time of year – so much so that a couple have been immortalised in song. The **holly** and the **ivy**, when they are both full-grown, will put out their fruit in November: the blood-red berries (technically 'drupes') of female holly trees and the clusters of small black berries that follow the ivy flowers with their unique smell. Both are important winter food for birds and small mammals; ivy berries are particularly calorie-rich, with nearly as many as a Mars bar, gram for gram. Keep an eye on your nearest ivy 'tod' (the name for a large clump of mature ivy): you'll likely see blackbirds and thrushes feasting on the berries, helping to keep them alive through winter, while the

dense evergreen foliage shelters many small birds through freezing winter nights. If you're out after dark and the skies are clear, look up: November to March is the best time for admiring the **Orion constellation**, which begins to appear high enough in the evenings to clear the roofline (in summer he appears in daytime, so is invisible). Orion is also known as The Hunter, and even if you know nothing about astronomy, you really can't miss him: look for three bright stars in a tilted line which make up his belt.[2] In his raised hands he holds a bow and – to the right – either a shield or a slain animal (mythological artists' interpretation varies); from his belt hangs a sword, the middle point of which is a vast and beautiful nebula, a cloud of gases and dust that's visible to the naked eye. The reddish star Betelgeuse ('Beetlejuice') marks one shoulder and due to its recent erratic behaviour it's thought that this supergiant, 800 times bigger than our sun, may explode into a supernova in the near future. If that happens in our lifetimes, it could be bright enough to be visible during the day.

Between dusk and midnight, you might hear the wavering '*hoo-hoooo*' of a male **tawny owl** – especially on clear, dry nights with a good moon. These gorgeous mottled brown hunters establish a 'home range' in late autumn, which a pair will then defend through the winter – hence all the racket. They live in woodland, including suburban parks with mature trees and even in central London (though there are none at all in Ireland) and hunt largely by perching, looking and listening downwards (their ears are at different

---

2 The second most obvious constellation in the sky is The Plough, which is visible all year round. These days I think most of us would compare its shape more readily to a saucepan, or perhaps a wok. If you take the two stars forming the opposite end of the pan to the handle and follow them northwards you'll find Polaris, the North Star.

heights, allowing them to pinpoint sound exactly) – then dropping and clamping their strong talons on to their prey like thunderbolts. The '*tu-whit, tu-whoo*' sound we think of them making is actually formed from the calls of both a male and a female: the female's contact call is better described as '*ke-WICK!*', after which the male often responds with his characteristic hoot. Tawnies mostly hunt small mammals such as voles and mice, but they're pretty adaptable (hence being able to live in some urban areas) and have been known to eat frogs, goldfish, large insects and even bats. They nest in cavities in trees but also like a good owl box, and tend to breed and lay their eggs relatively early in the year.

Not that there'll be many **bats** around from now on. November is the month in which they usually find somewhere with a stable temperature and tuck themselves away until spring; there are so few flying insects around over winter that if they didn't hibernate, they'd starve (depending on the weather, hedgehogs often stay active for a little bit longer as they can find invertebrates in leaf litter and on the ground). Winter roosts vary by bat species, but most UK bats, like tawny and little owls, roost and hibernate in hollows in trees – another reason why it's so important to leave standing dead timber. Some species will also nest in houses and other buildings like churches, in disused railway tunnels, or even, in the case of greater and lesser horseshoe bats, in caves – anywhere where the temperature remains stable and they'll be left alone.

I love bats. I grew up in a house with brown long-eared bats in the attic and I was absolutely fascinated by them, tucked into the rafters, their huge ears hanging down. I remember feeling so proud that our house was home to another species; I felt as though it was our job to keep them safe. But while that house still stands, I'm willing to bet the colony isn't there any more. Bats have suffered huge declines in this country due to a perfect storm of human-caused problems, including insect declines, pesticides and chemicals used in agriculture and as house timber treatments, increasing light pollution (including security lights and decorative garden lights) and growing numbers of pet cats.

Within reason (no indoor rodents, thanks), I want my cottage and its garden to be home to as many other creatures as possible. Even so, I was concerned about what I'd find when it was time to have my roof, lined only with 200-year-old reeds, insulated and waterproofed. All bat roosts are protected by law, and quite right too. The Bat Conservation Trust gave me some excellent advice on when best to have the work done, how to watch for bats entering and exiting, and which timber treatments wouldn't harm them, if it turned out I had woodworm; I also got my builder to come and have a careful look under the tiles well in advance of work starting so as to make sure there was no guano indicating a roost. Once the work was done I installed a bat box, and I'm incredibly proud to say that, going by the tiny black droppings that appeared on the windowsill below it, by the following winter it was occupied.

Out in the wider countryside, some bigger mammals are disappearing for winter, too. Across the UK, most cattle will spend the colder months under cover, eating fodder harvested earlier in the year and stored as hay, haylage or silage. Grass doesn't grow much over winter, so this stops pastures being nibbled bare and trampled to mud. If you live in an area of the countryside with lots of dairy or beef farming, you'll notice the **empty fields**. It can make the landscape feel oddly unoccupied.

There are compensations, though. November is peak season for **mist**, one of the subtler weather phenomena but one which gives me all sorts of interestingly melancholic feelings – perhaps because it can hide some of the more

obvious marks of human activity
on the landscape, or maybe just
because it acts to defamiliarise
a view, as snow does, making me
look properly at how beautiful it
is. Depending on the overnight weather
conditions, on still winter mornings tiny water droplets
can hang suspended in the air forming what is, in effect, a
cloud that hugs the ground. From this milky layer, skeletal
trees emerge like wraiths; it gathers in damp hollows or even
traces the shape of long-lost rivers, hinting at history and re-
enchanting the land.

Each day, note down the very best thing you experienced in the natural world.

Date

Date

Date

Date

Date

Date

First frost Date: _____   Took frost photos

BIRD BY EAR

Male starlings sing all year except when they're
in moult, but in winter their numbers are swelled
by visitors from chilly northern Europe, giving
us more opportunities to hear them perform.
Have a listen to one using an app or online (see
Resources): as well as having an extraordinary
repertoire of sounds, from rapid clicks to buzzes
to wolf whistles, they are skilled mimics[1] and will
casually throw into their recital the '*bip-bip*' when
someone locks their car, a phone ringtone or
snatches of other birds' song. If you hear something
from a nearby aerial that sounds like either a frisky
builder or R2-D2, that'll be a starling.

1 As Mozart found
when he whistled
a few bars to one
in a pet shop.
He purchased it
immediately, and it
lived with him for
three years.

☐ *Leafless oak*   ☐ *Seed balls on plane tree*

Dissolve owl pellets in warm water with a bit of washing-up liquid, then pick the tiny bones and/ or bits of insect exoskeleton from the water, using tweezers or your fingers. Rinse carefully, then lay them on tissue paper to dry. Owl pellet charts online will help you work out what the owl had preyed on.

Leaf litter: good
Litter: not so much

 ☐ *Scarlet holly berries* ☐ *Flaming dogwood stems*

Date

Date

Date

Date

Date

Date

☐ *Wild clematis seed heads*

Date

Date

Date

Date

Date

Date

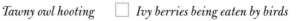 ☐ *Tawny owl hooting* ☐ *Ivy berries being eaten by birds*

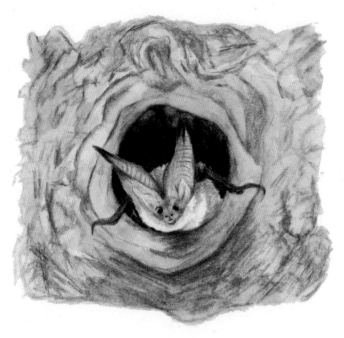

Natterer's bats hibernate in winter

Get into the habit of scanning mud, frost and snow for animal prints: they can be a great clue to what goes on when you're not there. Fox prints are oval and often left in a neat line; badger prints are broad and widely spaced, with five toes and long claws. Deer leave paired slots ranging from those left by muntjac, only 3–4cm long, to red deer at up to 9cm.

☐ *Detritivores (woodlice etc) in leaf litter*

Tawny owl

Be brave and boost your stores of inner grit by experiencing nature in all weathers. Watch how plants, insects and animals respond to rain, wind and cold; learn how your local green spaces change depending on the conditions.

🔍 ☐ *Orion with his belt, sword and nebula* ☐ *Low-lying mist*

Date

Date

Date

Date

Date

Date

Date

Date

Date

Birds love ivy berries

🔍 *BONUS* ☐ *Last bat of the year* ☐ *Cattle pasture empty*

Date

Date

Date

*Look for faint trails through grass and openings
in hedges: these are likely to be made by wild
creatures, which tend to stick to familiar
routes. With permission, they are good places
to set a trailcam, or you could simply find
a good spot to sit at dusk, and wait.*

December

Stillness and survival as
we approach the year's
chill midnight: the shortest
day, the longest night

Once again, we wake in darkness, and it's dark when we finish work for the day. Even at its peak, the sun is low in the sky and generates little heat. The ground retains no more warmth from summer, and can freeze hard and very deep. Little grows: the living sap is way down in trees' stems and trunks. Perennial plants sleep in the cold soil; the eggs and pupae of next year's insects hide in insulating leaf litter and under bark. Everything is hunkered down, still, and in survival mode.

Try imagining June right now, when the grass was tall and lush, the trees were in leaf, the world was full of insects and the evenings were warm and long: it's almost impossible. Winter can feel, in its dim, dark depths, like a completely different world. It wouldn't be true to claim there's as much to see outdoors as there was at midsummer: with so much less energy coming from the sun there's little plant growth, which means a vast reduction in insect activity and a knock-on effect from both things on birds, mammals, amphibians and reptiles, and pretty much everything else – including us.

Like badgers, like foxes, we too retreat to our dens: curtains closed, telly on, damp scarf and bobble hat on a hook by the door. The shops are playing festive hits, there's *Strictly* on the telly and presents to wrap – but despite all the focus on the indoor world and Christmas, I urge you to get outside on fine days and keep your body and mind connected to December, just as you've done for every month of the year so far.

One of my winter rituals is to **make a wreath** for my front door. Some people go all-out on wreath-making and you can find amazing tutorials online or even sign up for a workshop. My wreaths tend to be very simple and usually wonky, and I love them all the more for that. A few years ago, I bought a wicker ring from eBay as a base, and I reuse it year after year. I go out for a walk, usually around December 15th, with a canvas tote and secateurs, and harvest bits of holly, ivy and anything else green, making sure it's not from someone's front garden, and also making sure, if I snip any berries, that I leave as much as possible for the birds. Then I bring it all home and lay it out on the living room rug, pour myself a drink and haphazardly start to poke the stems into the wicker base, securing them with string or wire. I save the bits with berries until last, so they're on top, and then I hang it on my door. It usually lasts into January, though I sometimes top it up if bits fall off.

I really feel that it's important to mark the **winter solstice**, which falls a few days before Christmas: just as important as marking midsummer, maybe even more so, given that this can feel like such a dark time of year. If, like the writer Josie George, you pressed some flowers at midsummer, the winter solstice is the day to open up the press and enjoy them again. You might want to go for a dawn or dusk walk, light a candle or – if you can do it safely – build a small bonfire. Take a moment to experience midwinter in heart, head, body and soul, because from now onwards, the light little by little will begin to return. It won't be long now until the first snowdrops open, and the extraordinary, grand, spectacular pageant cranks itself up again.

For now, while there's less growth and change in the natural world than there is in summer, there's still a lot out there to enjoy. For one thing, it's a good time for photography: a low winter sun – only 15 degrees above the horizon at midwinter, compared to 60-odd degrees at midsummer – has a gorgeous, warm cast that comes from having to pass through more of the Earth's atmosphere, during which the bluer light is scattered. Given the right conditions, in midwinter, '**golden hour**' can seem to last all day.

If there's a *really* hard freeze overnight, there's the possibility of beautiful, fern-like **Jack Frost patterns** on my car windows (and, sometimes, on my cottage windows too). These form in conditions where the air is full of moisture and the temperature falls very low. Microscopic bits of dust or imperfections on the glass become hubs for frost as it grows outwards from each point, causing it to spin off into beautiful fractal geometries.

If you're out at night in the middle of December it's worth keeping an eye out for falling stars. The **Geminids meteor shower** is one of the most spectacular of the yearly events, starting close to December 4th and peaking around December 15th; the best time to look is in the wee small hours, when the sky is at its darkest, but you're pretty likely to see one at a more amenable time if you can get away from street lights (and the moon, if it's full) and are happy to hang around for a bit. The meteors don't travel as fast as in some other showers, making them easier to spot, and what's more, they seem to be getting more prolific: good news for skygazers who don't have fancy equipment and would prefer not to be out all night.

By day, there's not a lot of birdsong to enjoy in December. Most birds save their singing for breeding season: as you know, spring is when the dawn chorus (and evening chorus) happen, with song tailing off in summer and in all but a couple of cases, falling silent as birds moult in August, not to return until temperatures rise again. **Robins**, however, sing almost all year round to defend their territories – both males and females too. They can be fierce in defence of their home patch, and fights can go on to the death. Listen out for your local robins and if you can, help them get through winter by feeding them some dried mealworms, which you can get from pet food shops or garden centres – especially if the night-time temperatures get really low. And don't forget to put water out for the birds each morning if everything freezes.

However, birds don't just sing, they make sounds to raise the alarm or keep in contact with one another. The **mistle thrush**, which looks like a slightly fatter version of the spotty-chested song thrush, has a completely unique alarm call that's usually described as being like a wooden football rattle; however, this description needs updating, as – let's be honest – hardly anyone knows what one of those is these days. I used to see mistle thrushes regularly from the top deck of my bus to and from work when I lived in south London, and one day I got off a few stops early to see what they were. That's when I first heard their rattling alarm call and began to explore the little park alongside my bus route that would eventually become a key location in my first novel. I still think of mistle thrushes with great affection today.

They're known as 'mistle' thrushes due to their love of another winter staple: **mistletoe**. These balls of leaves and berries occur in mature trees and are semi-parasitic – though it would take a lot of them to harm their host. The sticky white berries, which appear in winter, are a favourite of mistle thrushes, which then poo the seeds out (or wipe their beaks on a nearby branch), thus 'planting' them on other trees. But here's the interesting thing: while the mistle thrush is on the Red List, with numbers down by 58 per cent between 1967 and 2020, in recent years, some areas of the country have seen an upturn in mistletoe. This strange plant is very difficult to germinate on trees by hand, and had been on the wane here since we got rid of most of our old apple orchards, one of its favourite hosts. The reason is thought to be climate change, albeit indirectly: milder winters have allowed more and more blackcaps to spend the winter here instead of just

 visiting for spring and summer, and yep, you've guessed it: blackcaps love mistletoe berries too.

The bleak midwinter is the time when some bird species gather together in huge flocks to roost at night, keeping one another warm, making it harder for predators to pick one off, and sharing information about good feeding spots. Even tiny wrens get seriously sociable on cold nights, with one record of sixty-three birds seen popping out of a single garden nest box, like corks from a bottle. But there are two species that have really got the whole mass-winter roost thing down to a fine art, and while one is known for its spectacular displays, the other you could walk within feet of and not know anything about.

There are three kinds of wagtail in the UK: pied (sometimes called 'white' on international sites and apps), grey (grey back, yellow bib; likes water) and yellow (a rare summer visitor, bright sulphur and olive-green). It's the pied wagtail most of us will be familiar with: black and white with a long tail which it wags up and down constantly; hangs around in urban areas and supermarket car parks picking tiny insects from the tarmac. The poet John Clare called it 'little trotty wagtail', while more recently it's been dubbed 'the Chiswick flyover' for its habit of tweeting '*chizzick!*' as it flies overhead.

Pied wagtails often gather together into night-time roosts which can swell in winter to number in the hundreds or, in some cases, the thousands. These might be in natural areas that provide some protection, like thickets of gorse or reed beds, but they do sometimes form in city centres, which can be warmer than the surrounding countryside. For decades there was a famous roost of an estimated 3,600 pied wagtails in some plane trees on O'Connell Street in Dublin, a spectacle that only came to an end when the trees were cut down; around 3,000 were once counted roosting in a supposedly bird-proofed area just outside Heathrow's Terminal 5, and 4,300 in some dense laurel bushes outside Orpington station in Kent. Once the birds were in place they would fall completely silent, and you could pass within feet of them, never knowing they were there.

Mass **wagtail roosts** can be hard to find, though a carpet of small bird droppings on the ground below is a good giveaway. Social media and your local press can be good sources of info, or if you're out doing Christmas shopping at around 3.30–4pm, keep your eyes peeled for lots of small, long-tailed birds flying into the same street tree or bank of bushes.

Starlings' cold-weather roosting behaviour is a lot more flamboyant. Their dawn and dusk **murmurations** – when large numbers form billowing clouds that shape-shift spectacularly – have long been a staple of wildlife television and in recent years, photos and videos of them have been doing decent numbers on social platforms, too; there's even a website, www.starlingsintheuk.co.uk, set up to help people find and see this uniquely Insta-friendly spectacle. But I don't think the recent interest in murmurations is just about uploading content and racking up views; I think our growing awareness that there's simply so much less of everything than there once was makes the seeming abundance of a huge flock of birds emotionally reassuring – no matter that starlings are now on the UK's Red List due to steep and continuing falls in their breeding population here. I also think that without always knowing it, we're increasingly nature-deprived and starved of spectacle. Seeing (and hearing) a flock of birds that huge, doing something amazing that has nothing at all to do with us, is exhilarating, and I believe it activates something wild and wonderful deep in our basal ganglia – or our collective unconscious, if you prefer.

Communal winter roosts begin to form when the weather gets really cold and are usually established by December, with starling numbers further boosted this month by millions of birds that come to the UK to escape harsher conditions further east. Once a roost is established, its exact position can vary slightly, from one area of reed bed to a neighbouring one (as at Leighton Moss in Lancashire), or from one side of a pier (for example Brighton's derelict West Pier) to the other. Added to that, the 'sky patterns' don't always happen; sometimes, groups of birds simply fly in and take their places in the roost. This element of unpredictability can make murmuration viewing trickier than some people expect, but it also adds to the euphoria when you find yourself at last in just the right position to see one, or the whole flock passes directly overhead.

Have you ever seen the Northern Lights? Amazingly, you don't have to go to Iceland: the **aurora borealis**, as they're properly called at our latitude, can sometimes be seen from the UK, including the southern counties. There's no peak month for spotting them, but the darker-for-longer skies of winter give you a better chance. Download one of the aurora-watching apps (see Resources) and sign up to receive alerts; be aware that you might need to be ready to travel away from bright lights, or wait until the darkest part of the deep, December night.

Keep your eyes peeled, too, for rare **nacreous clouds**: these occur at extremely high altitude and are formed of tiny ice crystals, much smaller than those which occur in ordinary clouds. When the sun is a few degrees below the horizon it lights them from below, diffracting the light in such a way as to create iridescence. They are only seen from the UK when the air that circulates high above the Poles is temporarily displaced.

I've said before that the unpredictability and even the 'inconvenience' of nature is one of the things that does us the most good: despite the deep changes we've wrought on the places animals call home, we're not in charge of what happens when, and many trips to see and hear things won't work out. But if we could order up nature like a Netflix box set, the value of each precious and hard-won encounter would be so much less.

Each day, note down the very best thing you experienced in the natural world.

Date

Date

Date

Date

Date

Date

○ ☐ *Geminids meteor shower*   ☐ *Robin singing*

BIRD BY EAR

Although you can hear robins singing almost all year
round, now is the best time to learn to recognise
them as most other species have fallen silent, save for
the wren, our bird by ear for next month. But while
wrens' songs are loud and rapid-fire, the robin's
is very different: languid, silvery and melancholy,
composed of distinct phrases that tail off as though
unfinished, then a pause, and then another poignant
attempt to tell the same, affecting tale.

For hundreds of years people on these islands decorated their homes with evergreen foliage at Christmas, rather than tinsel. Holly, ivy, fir trees and mistletoe represent life at the year's lowest point, and gathering them is a good excuse to get outdoors. Make sure you leave enough to act as food and habitat, though.

Jack Frost makes magic at night

 ☐ *Mistle thrush alarm call* ☐ *Mistletoe ball in a tree*

Date

Date

Date

Date

Date

Date

Date

Date

Date

Date

Date

Date

 ☐ *Made a door wreath*   ☐ *Jack Frost patterns*

Mistletoe is a parasite, albeit a pretty one!

Be in your body, not just your head. Feel how it responds, whether it's the way trees help your shoulders drop, or how the smell of petrichor slows your breathing. If you know where you hold stress – perhaps your neck, jaw, shoulders or gut – notice which natural experiences ease the tension.

A heart-stopping murmuration

Start to notice the wind direction and how it affects weather: winds from the north are generally colder than those from the south. Check your weather app, and then go out and feel the difference on your skin. Eventually you won't need the app to tell you when it's shifted!

Took photos at 'golden hour'

Date

Date

Date

Date

Date

Date

☐ *Marked the winter solstice, the shortest day*

Date

Date

Date

A home-made wreath

 BONUS ☐ *Pied wagtail mass roost* ☐ *Nacreous cloud*

Date

Date

Date

Date

> *If you feel yourself drawn to a particular tree, bird, wildflower or other creature, go with it. Read up about it, visit it as often as you can, and watch it change through the seasons. Build a relationship with it, and enjoy having it in your life.*

☐ *Watched a starling murmuration*   ☐ *Spotted the aurora borealis*

A COMMENCEMENT
ADDRESS

Instead of a conclusion, I wanted to offer you a
commencement address, as graduates of this course.

For every moment we exist on this living, breathing, still
welcoming planet, we are surrounded by stories and processes
and forces both deeply familiar and utterly unknown. From
the daisies opening their 'day's eyes' on your lawn to the
complex migrations of millions of birds, from the unfolding
of a new dragonfly's fragile four wings to an awe-inspiring
shimmer of colours far out in space, we live among miracles
we have somehow forgotten to enjoy.

With each new year of noticing, learning, remembering
and caring, you're building a deeper, truer, more meaningful
relationship with the natural world you move through, one
whose benefits will flow strongly both ways. I hope you'll
always carry it with you, folding it into all the months and
years to come: a new life, full of everyday wonders.

May you always know that nature is your home.

RESOURCES

Bookshelf

Adams, Jane V., *Nature's Wonders: Moments that Mark the Seasons* (National Trust Books, 2023)

Bang, Preben and Dahlstrom, Preben, *Animal Tracks and Signs* (Oxford University Press, 2001)

Beattie, Rebecca, *The Wheel of the Year: Your Rejuvenating Guide to Connecting with Nature's Seasons and Cycles* (Elliott & Thompson, 2023)

Beer, Andy, *Every Day Nature: How Noticing Nature Can Quietly Change Your Life* (National Trust Books, 2020)

Bradbury, Kate, *One Garden Against the World: In Search of Hope in a Changing Climate* (Bloomsbury Wildlife, 2024)

Bradbury, Kate, *The Bumblebee Flies Anyway: A Year of Gardening and Wild(Life)* (Bloomsbury Wildlife, 2018)

Bradbury, Kate, *Wildlife Gardening: For Everyone and Everything* (Bloomsbury Wildlife, 2019)

Chapman, Kiera; Jaines, Rowan; Ellender, Lulah and Warren, Rebecca, *Nature's Calendar: The British Year in 72 Seasons* (Granta Books, 2023)

Cohu, Will, *Out of the Woods: The Armchair Guide to Trees* (Short Books, 2015)

Crumley, Jim, *The Nature of Autumn* (Saraband, 2016)

Crumley, Jim, *The Nature of Spring* (Saraband, 2019)

Crumley, Jim, *The Nature of Summer* (Saraband, 2020)

Crumley, Jim, *The Nature of Winter* (Saraband, 2017)

Gallagher, Kirsty, *Sacred Seasons: Nature-Inspired Rituals, Wisdom and Self-Care for Every Day of the Year* (Yellow Kite, 2023)

Gooley, Tristan, *The Secret World of Weather: How to Read Signs in Every Cloud, Breeze, Hill, Street, Plant, Animal and Dewdrop* (Sceptre, 2021)

Harrison, Melissa (editor), *Autumn: An Anthology for the Changing Seasons* (Elliott & Thompson, 2016)

Harrison, Melissa (editor), *Spring: An Anthology for the Changing Seasons* (Elliott & Thompson, 2016)

Harrison, Melissa (editor), *Summer: An Anthology for the Changing Seasons* (Elliott & Thompson, 2016)

Harrison, Melissa (editor), *Winter: An Anthology for the Changing Seasons* (Elliott & Thompson, 2016)

Heisman, Rebecca, *Flight Paths: How the Mystery of Bird Migration Was Solved* (Swift Press, 2023)

Howard, Jules, *The Wildlife Pond Book: Create Your Own Pond Paradise for Wildlife* (Bloomsbury Wildlife, 2019)

Johnson, Owen and More, David, *Collins Tree Guide* (Collins, 2006)

Jones, Lucy, *Losing Eden: Why Our Minds Need the Wild* (Allen Lane, 2020)

Leendertz, Lia, *Almanac: A Seasonal Guide* (Gaia, new publication each year)

Lewis, James Weston and Thomas, Emily, *The Wild Handbook: Seasonal Activities to Help You Reconnect with Nature* (Studio Press, 2021)

Mabey, Richard, *Flora Britannica* (Chatto & Windus, 1996)

Mabey, Richard and Cocker, Mark, *Birds Britannica* (Chatto & Windus, 2020)

Mabey, Richard and Marren, Peter, *Bugs Britannica* (Chatto & Windus, 2010)

Newton, Ian, *Bird Migration* (Collins, 2010)

Packham, Chris, *Chris Packham's Nature Handbook: Explore the Wonders of the Natural World* (Dorling Kindsersley, 2022)

Parikian, Lev, *Into the Tangled Bank: Discover the Quirks, Habits and Foibles of How We Experience Nature* (Elliott & Thompson, 2021)

Rackham, Oliver, *The History of the Countryside: The Classic History of Britain's Landscape, Flora and Fauna* (Weidenfeld & Nicholson, 2020)

Richardson, Miles, *Reconnection: Fixing Our Broken Relationship with Nature* (Pelagic Publishing, 2023)

Rose, Francis, *The Wild Flower Key: How to Identify Wild Plants, Trees and Shrubs in Britain and Ireland* (Warne, 2006)

Sheldrake, Merlin, *Entangled Life: How Fungi Make Our Worlds, Change Our Minds and Shape Our Futures* (Bodley Head, 2020)

Steer, Rosie, *Slow Seasons: A Creative Guide to Reconnecting with Nature the Celtic Way* (Bloomsbury Publishing, 2023)

Sterry, Paul, *Collins Complete Guide to British Wildlife* (Collins, 2008)

Tree, Isabella, *Wilding: How to Bring Wildlife Back – An Illustrated Guide* (Macmillan, 2024)

Useful websites

www.bats.org.uk: Good advice from the Bat Conservation Trust on living alongside our brilliant bats, plus bat walks and events.

www.bbka.org.uk: The British Beekeepers Association. Help with all your bee swarm needs.

www.bsbi.org: The Botanical Society of Britain and Ireland organises the New Year Plant Hunt and publishes the Plant Atlas, a comprehensive guide to what grows where.

www.bto.org: The British Trust for Ornithology website is the best place for detailed information on the UK's birds. Includes live migration blogs in spring and autumn and cuckoo tracking.

www.buglife.org.uk: Help with identifying invertebrates, plus lots of information and advice on how to help pollinators and other insects.

www.butterfly-conservation.org: Information to help identify butterflies, from the organisation behind the Big Butterfly Count.

www.field-studies-council.org: Brilliant fold-out ID guides and nature-based courses.

www.gardenwildlifehealth.org: Report sick or dead birds or animals you find in your garden to help understand wildlife diseases and prevent outbreaks. In some cases, you may be asked to send in the carcass; they'll advise you on how to do that.

www.leaf.eco: The Linking Environment and Farming site is your port of call to learn about Open Farm Sunday in June.

www.naturespy.org: The best place to buy wildlife cameras, this non-profit ploughs money back into conservation. There's lots of useful advice too.

www.plantatlas2020.org: A vast, comprehensive survey of the plants of Britain and Ireland, also accessible via the BSBI website.

www.plantlife.org.uk: Find out which plants and fungi need our help, learn about specialist ecosystems and get involved with campaigns like No Mow May.

www.beta.slowways.org: This is a brilliant project which aims to create a network of tested walking routes connecting towns, villages and cities across the UK. Use it to plan walks or volunteer to test some local pathways.

www.stagbeetles.ptes.org/stag-beetle-count: Here's where to record your stag beetle sightings and help conserve these amazing critters.

www.starlingsintheuk.co.uk: Good info on where to see a starling murmuration near you during the colder months.

www.treecouncil.org.uk: Research, information, advice and campaigns celebrating trees and hedgerows, including for young people.

www.woodlandtrust.org.uk: 'Nature's Calendar' on the website is an interactive phenology calendar tracking key UK species through the year. A good way to find out how each season is unfolding.

www.wildlifetrusts.org: Find your nearest Wildlife Trust site and search for local nature news, guided walks, volunteering opportunities and outdoor activities, including events for kids.

www.xeno-canto.org: A great site for listening to professional recordings of birdsong and calls from all over Europe and beyond.

People to follow

If you're on social media, consider rewilding your feed with posts from some interesting and inspiring nature lovers. And for news about the wildlife in your area, follow your local park or its friends' society, your nearest nature reserve, Wildlife Trust site and birders' group:

- Nick Acheson (@themarshtit / @thewillowtit)
- Jane V Adams (@wildlifestuff / @janevadams)
- BBC Wildlife Magazine (@WildlifeMag / @bbcwildlifemagazine)
- Kate Bradbury (@Kate_Bradbury / @katebradbury)
- James Common (@commonbynature)
- Gert Corfield (@birdergwc64)
- Trevor Dines (@DrTrevorDines / @trevor.dines)
- Phil Gates (@durham_country_diarist)
- Josie George (@porridgebrain)
- Cath Hodsman (@CathHodsman)
- Richard Jones (@bugmanjones)
- Ali McKernan (@the.fungi.guy)
- Stephen Moss (@StephenMoss_TV)
- @naturalcalendar
- Lev Parikian (@LevParikian)
- Chris Reeve (@helminghamwildman)
- Steve Rutt (@steverutt / @steve.rutt)
- Amy Schwartz (@lizardschwartz)
- Megan Shersby (@meganshersby)
- Brigit Strawbridge (@B_Strawbridge / @brigitstrawbridge1)
- Ajay Tegala (@ajaytegala)
- Lira Valencia (@outsidewithlira)
- @virtualastronomer
- @wildflowerhour (also #wildflowerhour)
- Rob Yaxley (@rob_yaxley and @robert_yaxley)

Apps

AuroraWatch UK (free, iOS): Created by the Space and Planetary Physics group at Lancaster University's Department of Physics. This uses your location to alert you if the aurora borealis is likely to be visible where you are. You can also view webcams on the Shetland Isles to see any activity there.

Big Butterfly Count (free): From Butterfly Conservation, this app comes into its own during the annual citizen science project, helping you identify butterflies and moths, submit your records and see the results on an interactive map.

British Tree Identification (free): Made by The Woodland Trust, this app uses an identification key system (a series of questions) to narrow down results, rather than AI.

Bugs Matter (free): If you have access to a car, download this app and, each summer, record your bug splatters at the end of each journey. You'll be helping scientists monitor insect numbers.

Encounter (free): In development by yours truly, Encounter will be a guided nature journal for your phone. Record your notes as text, audio, photos or voice-to-text and receive alerts and info about what the natural world is up to all through the year: www.encounter-nature.com

Flora Incognita (free): Dated design but super-reliable results from this German-made plant ID app, a collaboration between several European research institutes. Usefully, it saves your identifications to a list for you to refer to again later.

Go Jauntly (free trial then £1.99 per month): Particularly good in urban areas, this walking app is packed with user-created routes and includes lots of photos. £1.99 a month means you can download routes for offline use or export them as GPX files. Includes a nature notes feature.

iNaturalist (free): Help with identifying plants and animals from a friendly international community and the chance to contribute to citizen science projects and research studies. The AI-powered Seek app is from the same developers and lets you earn badges and points.

Merlin Bird ID (free): The best birdsong recognition app currently available, created by the Cornell Lab of Ornithology using the vast eBird database. Install the correct data pack for your region and make sure location services are turned on.

Ordnance Survey (£34.99 per year or £6.99 per month): The UK's best mapping app; in fact, I'd say the world's. The level of detail is astonishing but most importantly, rights of way are marked in green so you can be sure you're allowed to be wherever you are.

Star Walk (free): This is such a clever window on the skies. It uses augmented reality to show you stars, planets and constellations, and help you find deep sky objects and even satellites.

Swift Mapper (free): Record swifts and their nest sites in order to help protect them during building work and renovations and help slow their decline.

ACKNOWLEDGEMENTS

I've had dozens of knowing and unknowing teachers in recent years, among them Kate Bradbury, Richard Mabey, Phil Gates, Jules Howard, Paul Evans, Megan Shersby, Chris Reeve, Amy Schwartz, James Common, Jane Adams and David Darrell-Lambert: thank you for sharing your nature knowledge so generously and widely and well.

Thank you also to my dauntless agent, Jenny Hewson, and to my editor Alexa von Hirschberg, whose vision this book largely was, to Katie Crous and Claudia Dyer for their expert attention, Amanda Dilworth for her captivating illustrations, and Alice Graham, Cait Davies, Clarissa Sutherland, Frances Rooney, Hannah Owens, Helen Ewing, Helena Fouracre and Sian Smith at W&N, all of whom know how to turn words into things and put them into the hands of readers.

The paper and boards used for this book are uncoated, responsibly sourced and certified by the Forest Stewardship Council. All the inks are plant-based.

Melissa Harrison is a novelist and nature writer. She contributes a monthly Nature Notebook column to *The Times* and writes for the *FT Weekend*, the *Guardian* and the *New Statesman*. Her most recent novel, *All Among the Barley*, was the UK winner of the European Union Prize for Literature. It was a Waterstones Paperback of the Year and a Book of the Year in the *Observer*, the *New Statesman* and the *Irish Times*. Her previous books have been shortlisted for the Costa Novel Award and longlisted for the Women's Prize for Fiction (*At Hawthorn Time*) and the Wainwright Prize (*Rain*). She lives in Suffolk.